Pregnancy

in His Presence

Philippa-Jo C Dobson

ISBN-13: 978-1490917627
ISBN-10: 1490917624

Pregnancyinhispresence.com

facebook.com/pregnancyinhispresence

twitter.com/prespregnancy

Dedication

I would like to dedicate this book to my children, Beth-Annily, Reuben-River, for the one who got away and the one on the way. This is because of you and for you. The experiences of your births have birthed in me tenacity and faith, founded on His presence. You were my inspiration. May the height of the ground I have won become your starting point, may you go after and live in the good of all that He has won for you. May you always be marked by His presence and stand out from those around you.

Acknowledgements

A huge thank you to all who have made this project a reality. So many of you have taken time and effort to help me along this book writing journey. For all my friends and family who have taught me through their own experiences and who (unknowingly sometimes) have made an off-hand comment that has crafted the way I think, adding richness to this work. To my husband Luke, for continually believing in me and supporting me in my journeys through pregnancy, without you I wouldn't have been able to stand the test, you have held up my arms and continually do so. We make a great team.

But as cheesy as it sounds, right from the word go, I want to thank God most of all. You are the one that set this in motion and I am blown away that you would use me, of all people to write a book that would give me a voice among women and give me a platform to shout from. This journey is really about you and me and I have let others in to see our story, I know you won't mind! I'm love sick for you and can never get enough of you. You continually amaze me with your goodness, generosity and love for me.

Contents Page

Endorsements

"*Pregnancy in His Presence* is an essential addition to every family's personal library. Philippa-Jo glides effortlessly from tender personal testimonies to inspiring and motivating advice whilst laying a firm foundation of biblical truth which is accessible for all. She is a true spiritual midwife who is sure to help birth the Kingdom standard from conception through to childbirth and beyond for many women with the assistance of this anointed book and journal"

Rachel-Ann Ball **- mother of three**

"Philippa-Jo's book arrived in my inbox during this time of uncertainty and battling. It gave me biblical back up and practical applications to be able to stand on what I knew was God's heart for my baby and myself. It's an absolutely vital book shedding light on the truth of God's heart for every woman and baby in relation to childbirth."

Rhiannon **- mother of two**

"It was during my first pregnancy that I had the great privilege of reading the Pregnancy in His presence book and journal by Philippa-Jo Dobson. The journal provided me with a wonderfully practical resource for taking the supernatural promises of God and making them a reality ('on earth as it is in Heaven'). It is packed full of ideas and exercises that I was able to use to fully equip me both spiritually and emotionally for all that lay ahead. Not only did it help to prepare me for pregnancy and childbirth, most importantly it helped me to deepen my faith and my relationship with God. I thoroughly recommend the journal to all expectant mothers, it is written in such a way that enables the reader to use it for deep study and also to read it in small portions for regular doses of encouragement. Philippa-Jo unashamedly reveals the full measure of God's promises for pregnancy and childbirth and challenges the reader to settle for nothing less than God's best.

Philippa-Jo is a pioneer in this area, she writes from personal experience and shares the supernatural testimonies from both of her pregnancies and births. This enables her to speak with confidence and authority, which I found not only encouraging but also challenging. With the knowledge of all that God had done for Philippa-Jo, I knew that he could do it for me too.

Through reading the Pregnancy in His Presence book and journal and following the advice and guidance that Philippa-Jo gives I was able to enter the experience of childbirth fully prepared and resourced with my faith levels high, confident in the knowledge that God wanted to give me his best. With such assurance I could never have settled for anything less."

Lydia Porter - **mother of one**

"This book is full of sound advice mixed with Godly insights. How I wish I had been a follower of Jesus when I was pregnant with my children!"

Dwee Cooke - **Director of Streams Training Centre England,**

Pastor of The Bridge Church, Cheltenham

Foreword

Philippa-Jo is undeniably a woman of passion and insight and this brave book highlights her capacity for faith over and above what others would consider to be the norm. If you're having a baby or planning one, this book gives great insight in the role that focused faith can play in your pregnancy and labour. Jo is clear sighted and courageous in her capacity to show God's willingness to be involved with the business of having a baby.

It would be difficult to read this book without faith rising for a gestation and labour that borders on the supernatural. However, Jo is also open and honest about her own experience and acknowledges that the perfect may not be reached. However, as she explains, while you may not get all the great results you believed for, simply the practice of focused believing gives such good results that it's definitely worth doing.

Her encouragement to women to believe for something better than they may have experienced or heard of before is heartening, yet she does it with a grace that allows for something less than what was hoped for. This book is worth a read for all those who are willing to believe God to make the difference in the natural process of childbirth.

Bev Murrill **m.a.g.l.**

Executive Director of Christian Growth International
Director of Cherish Uganda
Author of: Catalysts: You can be God's agent for change
And: Speak life and shut the hell up...

1

An invitation:
Divine possibilities

Until I became pregnant for the first time, I had limited expectations of what the pregnancy and labour experience would be like. I had been washed over with all the normal presumptions about motherhood from many different sources. Television frequently portrays mothers going through nine months of discomfort, followed by long drawn out and very painful deliveries with all kinds of hideous complications. I have come to realise that although I was unaware of what my expectations were, even though I may not be aware of them, in all things I do have a viewpoint. These viewpoints are created from a range of places; television, books, the internet and word of mouth. If I do not have my guard up then negative thoughts can lead to negative expectations, without me even being aware that I am forming a viewpoint on each topic. In 2 Corinthians 10:5, it says that we are to 'take captive every thought to make it obedient to Christ'. I believe there needs to be a massive shift in the way that we and the

'Take captive every thought to make it obedient to Christ'

societies we live in view childbearing. I believe that it should be the job of the Church to be on the cutting edge of new revelation, in all spheres of life be it business or health, innovation or invention, we are called to have the mind of Christ and display His likeness to the world around us. My aim is to start a dialogue about childbearing that will spark a forest fire of conversation and in turn change the mindset of a generation's view towards childbearing. I intend to challenge understandings of pregnancy and labour that we have gleaned from living purely from our earthy perspective. I want to change the lenses of how we look at childbirth. I want you to discover what is available when we live from a heavenly perspective.

I discovered I was pregnant for the first time at exactly four weeks gestation, when being sick so often the previous week made me question my dates and take a pregnancy test. I was delighted to find I was pregnant but felt physically lousy and extremely tired. When my husband and I announced we were expecting our first child people asked me how I felt, I laughed and with a smile on my face said I felt sick, like it was a normal expected part of the journey. I enjoyed people's sympathy as a rite of passage into motherhood, I revelled in the fact that I was now part of the club. Looking back now that seems ridiculous. Why? Because the lenses I viewed childbearing with have changed.

At around my sixth week of pregnancy, a friend of mine gave me a book called, 'Supernatural Childbirth', by Jackie Mize.[1] It shifted my understanding of God's plan for childbirth. As I read the testimony of another ordinary woman, I understood that I had been believing several misconceptions about childbirth. I believed that I should be tired, sick, achy, swelling up in various places, in pain and getting stretch-marks. What I had discovered in the Bible and through Jackie Mize's testimony challenged these misconceptions which I now believe are lies of the enemy. It was now time to change my mindset and take off the lenses that were warping the Word of God. What I read humbled me, I decided that I would no longer default to the pattern of the world's thinking on childbearing but transform my view of childbearing by renewing my mind (Romans 12:2). I set my face like flint and decided, with God's help, to pursue what I found in His Word, until I saw His goodness in the land of the living (Isaiah 50:7, Psalm 27:13) even if it was not 'normal' in the world's standard. I simply had to trust His presence enough to lean into it. I would not let my negative perceptions dictate the outcome of my pregnancy. I started to change my expectations.

On the whole women are still wearing the lenses given to us by the fall in Genesis. In the garden of Eden when sin entered, it did more than separate man from God. Mankind and the earth became disconnected from His life and were cursed. Pain and death entered what God had made as good. The Bible tells us that Jesus took all our pain and sin on the cross and that we are redeemed from the curse. Christ redeemed us from the curse of the law by becoming a curse for us, for it is written: "Cursed is everyone who is hung on a pole." (Galatians 3:13) We are no longer under the curse if we accept the hand of Jesus to pull us into a new position with Him (Ephesians 2:6). Our new position is one of sonship, we are reconnected to God. But the cross was more than an act of restoring our relationship with God, redemption is a restoration of all things back to God's original purpose for them, (Colossians 1:15-20). We no longer have to live under the curse because God has broken it's power, by the power of what He did on the cross. He paid the price for the judgement of the curse and purchased men for God. The Bible also says that because of what Jesus did through dying we can now access heavenly realms, it says that we are seated in heavenly places with Christ (Ephesians 2:6). We know that in God's Kingdom of Heaven there is no sickness or pain (Revelations 21:2-6 and Revelations 22:2), we can enter into the benefit of these verses now because it was at the cross that all things were made new, (2 Corinthians 5:17). So, if we as believers are seated in heavenly places then the reality of Heaven should be more real to us than our earthly experience. Therefore, if we live from a heavenly perspective we can live healthy, pain free lives, even in childbearing. In Matthew 6:10 Jesus taught us how to pray "your kingdom come, your will be done, on earth as it is in Heaven." His kingdom of Heaven needs to become our earthly reality. We know that it is His will for us to live free from pain because we can see Heaven's pain-free reality. At the fall in Eden man was separated from God and could no longer walk with Him in the garden. When Jesus rose again the curtain dividing us from the Holy place in the temple was torn, it was a symbol that God had restored that intimate relationship between Himself and man once again. Through the work of the cross and resurrection there is no divide for those who choose to step into the access that Jesus made for them. We can walk once again in relationship with God and all the benefits that come from being His heir. The aim of this book is for you to discover what living in His Kingdom, Heaven on Earth, looks like for you in your pregnancy.

Because the veil has been lifted, we are called as Christians to live a supernatural standard - the standard of Heaven: to live in the good of all that Jesus won for us. We have access to be able to have children with a supernatural standard because we can have Heaven's standard now. When Jesus said "it is finished" on the cross (John 19:30), He did it all: it's a finished work of the cross, nothing is missing or lacking, He won it all when He died and gained us access to Heaven. Many people are now happy to accept that God heals, this is a marvellous revelation to the church and I am so excited to see God's healing hand moving often through His body. But when we put this healing principle in the same sentence as pregnancy I regularly see in return a shift in mindset, because of society's lenses to reflect not a heavenly standard but an earthly one based on the experience of sickness and pain in pregnancy and labour being the norm.

What you see in Heaven you can have on earth. (Matthew 6:10 and Matthew 18:18) I hope to help you to see what is available as Heaven's standard; but who am I to show you? Throughout this book I will tell you of my own experiences. I am a mother of two, and have one already with Jesus and one on the way, with all my pregnancies and both labours I believed and saw God do many amazing things, such as experiencing short deliveries, answered desires, a pain free labour and joyful laughter while delivering. I believe I have had births that were supernatural, surrounded by His presence. By choosing to live in a place of His presence I chose to lay down my circumstances and live in His glory, the Glory of Heaven where all is well with me (Proverbs 10:22). Did I get everything that I was believing for? No. However God revealed His standard to me and I got to live in some of it and go after what I didn't see for next time! The Christian life is a journey of discovering who God is who we are in Him and therefore what is available to us. We may not know at this point the fullness of what is available to us but we will know more tomorrow than we do today and more the day after than is revealed tomorrow, and so on. As we choose to spend time getting to know Him, we also get to know ourselves more and understand what He has called us to walk in. Do we always see the fullness of what He won for us today? Perhaps not, but we will see more of the fullness manifest in our lives tomorrow than we did today as we continually press into Him. As we become aware of Heaven around us, it changes the way we think and the way we think changes who we are. Our actions and responses flow out of who we are and those decisions and mindsets impact our outcomes. The key is His presence. Each time I've been pregnant I have had to process my previous experience and in some ways cast it off, wipe my slate clean, go back to the Word and decide that God is always right; I can go after again what I failed to see manifested last time. If you are reading this book, having come from a previous disappointment in childbearing, I have covered how to deal with disappointment in chapter 15 "Nothing Ventured, Nothing gained: How to deal with disappointment". Disappointment can rob our expectations and therefore rob us of living a heavenly standard the next time around.

God is not a respecter of titles, I am no different from the next woman. If you choose to search out what God has to say about your body, your baby, the finished work of His cross with His healing nature, and believe what you find there, then it is possible for you to enter into a happy healthy pregnancy. You can be strong and lively throughout with no sickness or disease in either you or your baby's body. You will be able to experience a joy-filled, short and painless labour. I hope that by the end of this book you will see the standard of Heaven and make it your life's goal to pursue it until you see it; not only in childbirth but throughout the whole of your life.

✦

2

Dream a little dream:

Hearing Gods plan

What does the Bible tell us about childbirth? We know from the scriptures that God intends for us to live pain free lives. (Examples of this can be found in 1 Chronicles 4:10, Isaiah 53:4 and Psalm 23:4.) Jesus on the cross paid the price and took ALL sickness upon Himself. So we can be free from morning sickness and every other pregnancy ailment that people try to tell us is normal. Colds and flu, in the world's standard, are 'normal' but as Christians we should be able to live free from them because Jesus has taken all sickness. Do we sometimes get colds? I do! But I don't feel like I've failed if I get one, it just shows me I'm not living in the standard of Heaven on a continual basis. Complete freedom from pain and sickness is the standard of what was won on the cross whether I live in it all the time or not.

Exodus 1:19 gives us a glimpse into what pregnant woman of the covenant were experiencing in Bible times. Now we, through Jesus, can enter into the same experience because we have an even greater covenant (Hebrews 7:22). "The Hebrew women are not like the Egyptian women," the midwives replied. "They are more vigorous and have their babies so quickly that we cannot get there in time."

Vigorous means, strong, healthy and full of energy. They gave birth quickly. That is what women of the covenant can experience, because of Jesus we have been grafted into His covenantal people, so we too can give birth in the same way as the Jewish women living in Egypt did. Giving birth in the way that the Jewish woman did was clearly not normal for the Egyptian woman just as suggesting a supernatural childbirth is not 'normal' today.

We are told repeatedly in scripture that we should live without fear and that His joy should be our strength. These scriptures do not exclude childbearing, so we should be full of joy and strength, living and thinking about pregnancy and labour without fear. Psalm 113:9 says, "He settles the barren woman in her home as a happy mother of children." Therefore we know that it is not God's intention for anyone to be barren. We also know that He is the author of life (Acts 3:15) so it is not His plan for anyone to miscarry (See also Psalm 1:3 and Malachi 3:11). Because of the work of the cross we know that God has taken all sickness and death, including deformity and disease, so under the heavenly standard no child should be born with either.

We limit ourselves by our limited understanding of how much power is in the cross

So we know from scripture that we can have children, we can be happy, we and our babies can be without aliment, sickness or pain, we can give birth quickly, without pain and live free from fear. These are amazing promises that we can stand on, if we choose to find them, and believe in the One who gave them. These things are all plainly in the Word and are non-negotiable, they are the standard of what the work of the cross won. Whoever you are and whatever your circumstance, you can stand on these truths and see them fulfilled in your pregnancy, and labour because Jesus paid the price for them. They are the standard experience of Heaven's reality, these things should be our 'normal'.

Does the Bible lay out clearly in one story or verse the blueprint for a 'supernatural' childbirth? No. You can choose to look at what I have laid out as far reaching, or explain away 'normal' birth as medical fact. Many people say that morning sickness shows that the pregnancy is healthy and medically it may do, but I'm suggesting that there is a higher way, a way that involves no sickness because we choose to pull on the standard of Heaven. We choose to believe in how powerful Jesus' death and resurrection was, we choose to believe that if Jesus took all pain then that means ALL pain, even in labour. When looking at the Exodus passage and believing for quick labour, it can be argued that it doesn't tell us how quick quickly was! It doesn't even say that the Hebrew woman had no pain. But if for a moment we can remove our lenses that have been put on from our worldly wash over of television and such, to look pragmatically and agree that by anyone's standard, over twelve hours of labour is long! If you decide to think that six hours is quick, or, for you it may be two hours, I think that God honours that faith. I am not suggesting a one size fits all package, this book and its accompanying journal are simply here for you to make up your own mind. You can decide what it is that you are expecting, what you think is available, and then I hope to help you to go after those things and also rest in the knowledge that the One who gave the promises is trustworthy.

For me, pulling all scripture together, drawing from the fact that God is good, I believe scripture does give us a blueprint, it does build a picture if you are willing to place all the pieces together like a puzzle. The pieces individually can be pulled apart and undermined but I think together the picture of the standard for pregnancy and labour is clear. Perhaps it is not specific in places, but it's from a place of relationship where you can walk out the details that a clear outline of no sickness, a pain-free and quick labour can be seen. It's as we develop this relationship with God that we can go after things that at the start of our journey with Him may have looked out of the question. For example, can we believe to have children without gaining stretch marks? It's out of a place of

How much do you think God cares about the small details of your life?

revelation in Him that we can go after things that may not be written in the Bible, but can be seen in the threads of His character.

How about other aspects, the things like "Shall I have a home birth?" or believing God that your baby will arrive at a certain time of day? These specifics on our 'What I am believing for' list are not outlined in scripture. So how do we know if we can have them or not?

Knowing God's will for your life with all the details, comes from relationship. Unless we spend time with God how can we know Him? If we don't know Him how can we know what He wants for us? If we don't know God we easily slip into believing lies about His character. If you don't know that God is good then you can easily doubt that He wants the best for you. If you question whether or not God wants you to experience His best, then you can start to believe that God is allowing pain or sickness into your life to teach you a lesson through those bad circumstances. This is a direct attack on His character because in fact, if we go back to the original truth, we know that God is good. And no good person would put us through pain to teach us something. So it is important for us to truly know His character. How do you get to know someone's character? By spending time with them. God is faithful to reveal Himself if we search Him out - "seek and you will find" (Matthew 7:7). So why not seek Him for our birthing experiences? God lives outside of time and knows the beginning from the end (Isaiah 46:10). Ask, what have we to lose? Find a quiet place and spend time with Him. It's a relationship so keep asking questions. What is God's plan for your pregnancy and birth? Ask Him. Using Week Seven of your journal and the additional pages at the rear of your journal write down what God says as you spend time with Him. Ask Him what His plan is for you. The standard remains the same, but our journeys are very different. All the promises of the Bible are available to you, the sickness and pain free elements have already been won for you so you know you can have them, but God wants you to have the desires of your heart too.

If when you spend time with Him you feel uneasy about something, or if you get a sense such as 'I'm going to have a c-section.' Ask God to clarify the details. God is not saying His plan is for us to have a caesarean, you know this because it does not reflect the goodness of His character or the sickness free reality He has won for us. It does not reflect the Bible either. If God is our healer then how can He harm? Sometimes I think God reveals an outcome as an opportunity to see if we will contend to see His Word performed in our lives. I believe if you hear something negative it is an opportunity to make a possible weakness into a strength. If we conquer fear in a particular area, it often becomes our biggest strength, (2 Corinthians 12:9 But He said to me, "My grace is sufficient for you, for my power is made perfect in weakness." Therefore I will boast all the more gladly about my weaknesses, so that Christ's power may rest on me). Using the above as an example, ask God "Why would I need to have a caesarean?" If He reveals to you that your baby is in the wrong position, or your cervix has ineffective dilation, then you know how and what to pray. By praying you can choose to change the outcome of your labour. Ask God again, "Is this your perfect plan for my labour?" Wait to hear His reply. You then have the knowledge of where your current situation is taking you and you have God's perfect plan for you. Then go into the Word and find scriptures that are relevant and pray them over yourself. Speak to your body using the knowledge you have and tell it to do what it needs to do. Then watch God be faithful to His Word and to you, His child. God is outside of time and knows the events of our lives. He would be able to see that if you remain on your current path you would need a caesarean. He reveals this to you and gives you the chance to change your future. You have a choice, you can accept what He tells you as His sovereign plan, or you can throw yourself back on His Word and see what His character is really like. Once you have seen His original design you can pray in His perfect will for you; you will not be negotiating God's plan, if you know Him and His Word, His plan for you never lowers from

I will lie down and sleep in peace, for you alone, O LORD, make me dwell in safety.

Psalm 4:8

Heaven's standard; pain and sickness free. If God shows you your current trajectory is in negative orbit then I believe it is not Him revealing His imperfect plan for you, because His plans are always perfect and for our good. It is therefore God helping you by pointing out your current course so that you can do something about it. It's God's goodness to tell you that you may be falling short of the standard; He wants you to succeed so He tells you so you have time to fix it before your labour. For example, when my children run ahead of me down the path, from my higher perspective I can see a pothole in the path in front of them, I call and warn them that if they carry on running on their current course they will fall over, I am not pointing it out so they run right into it! I am giving them the power and the information to change the outcome of their future by avoiding the hole. The same is true of Father God, He sees what lies ahead of us on our journey and gives us a heads up. So many Christians would say that when God reveals a negative outcome, it is God in His sovereignty preparing them, warning them that in the next few steps they will fall over and hurt themselves! - If my children don't listen to me and run straight into the pothole, I do not say, "well done you found it, that's exactly what I wanted to happen to you, now you know that life is hard, you've learnt a lesson," - this does not reflect a good and loving parent, and it is not what God does either. You pick your child up, brush them off, give them a kiss and say, "next time, listen when I tell you to avoid the hole."

God wants to reveal truth to you. The truth about your childbirth. Truth means reality. Truth is a person, Jesus. He wants to be involved in the process, He wants to reveal Himself to you, to be there for you. God wants to partner with you. How do we partner with God? As you hear His view on your childbirth, (He may speak to you, show you a picture, wash you with a feeling of peace or lead you to a scripture), you can now stand on these truths. The truth He reveals to you is specific, it's accurate because He is never wrong - you now have clear items and outcomes to believe for. Being specific helps you be sure and certain and therefore in faith (Hebrews 11:1). If you have a vague ideal outcome you can easily waver in your resolve as the lines around what you are believing become fuzzy. If someone, or circumstances, come and challenge that undefined belief because you have no sure boundary to what you are aiming for, it becomes all too easy for faith eventually to be non-existent. As you stand on firm, defined truth the reality of Heaven changes your earthly reality. Dwell on the truth in your thoughts, write them up and read them each day, tell someone else and agree together, pray through it every morning. Speak the truth over your body. His Word is placed above all things (Psalm 138:2). When God speaks things are created, when you speak His Word over your body you create an outcome. Your body must bow to a greater reality of truth. Remember truth is a person and every knee will bow to Him: Jesus (Philippians 2:10). God is the best birthing partner because He can already see the outcome of your pregnancy and labour. He is for you so what, or who, can be against you? Partner together with God and see the truth of Heaven become a reality in your life. Know God and know His plan for you. Do not be shy to ask. Be realistic about how you feel. Always take your fears and concerns back to Him who is the author and finisher of our faith, get back into His presence where you will find rest.

3

Wouldn't it be nice:

Drawing out your heart's desire

I had in my heart a list of things I wanted to see happen at both of my childbirths, some items came from spending time with God and others were things I wanted. Those lists developed as I got nearer to my due dates. In my second pregnancy I emailed my list to the small group of friends I trusted, so that they could pray in faith for what I was believing for.

Things like "I would like no pain" we know we can have because we have seen in the Bible that God's desire for us is to be pain free, to say less would negate the work of the cross as incomplete. Some of the other things on my list were 'wish list' items that would make me feel more comfortable, like a home birth. I don't think God really minds where we give birth but He does mind if we are comfortable. You are His daughter and He wants to bless you.

Have a think about what you would like to see in your pregnancy and labour. Read over your notes from spending time with God. Use the space in your journal to make your own "What I am believing for" list. Include everything you want to see happen, even if you think it is insignificant. God wants to give you the desires of your heart (Psalm 20:4). So, allow yourself to dream. I know this to be true. When I was sitting in the hospital for a routine check up during my first pregnancy a midwife I had never met stopped and talked so kindly to another pregnant woman that I thought to myself, "She would be lovely to have at my birth." The Lord heard my silent prayer and granted the unspoken desire of my heart. I laughed when she arrived half way through my labour. It let me understand that God really is interested in the details of what I would like.

So, we can ask for things that are 'wish list' items but our faith should not be rocked if we don't get them. Like if I didn't get my home birth or have that particular midwife it would not have mattered.

To make your own list like this you need to find for yourself what's in the Bible, what you can have. Don't take my word for it. It has to become known truth to you personally. Read the scriptures. (I have laid out just a few relevant verses in the "Scriptural Blueprints" chapter at the end of this book). Ask Holy Spirit to reveal the Word to you before you start reading, it is His job to make truth known to you. Find out for yourself what the Bible says you can have. Then spend time with Jesus and hear His personal plan for you. Find out anything you particularly need to apply the Word to, such as any hereditary family illness. (We are co-heirs with Jesus, grafted into His family, He broke the curse for us so our children can live in His bloodline, not our natural one). Spend time with Jesus as you write this list. Be conscious of His prompting. Try numbering or circling those things that you are absolutely certain of. Be honest with yourself and in another colour circle the things that you need more faith for. Underline the things that you have to have, leaving the things that are 'wish list' items without lines. For example using my list I would have underlined 'quick labour' but not 'ideally under an hour and a half.' Remember, be specific, dare to dream the impossible, set clear and obvious outcomes so that you know exactly what you are aiming for. That way you will not falter in your resolve to go after them. It will also be a great testimony when you see exactly what you were believing for happen in such specific detail.

Dear Girls,

Things on my wish list so you know what I'm praying for:

For me:
- *A quick labour: under three hours, ideally one and a half from first twinge to birth*
- *No more false labours (I've been up for two nights thinking..., "Is this it?")*
- *To go into labour naturally on my own before next Thursday*
- *No pain (Some of the false labours I've had have been hurting some times)*
- *No tearing, grazes, or swelling*
- *To push no more than ten times*
- *To have a home birth and stay at home after birth*

For baby:
- *To not ever be in stress*
- *Engage quickly*
- *To not poo in the amniotic fluid before he's born!*
- *Blood sugar levels to be normal*
- *Feed well and immediately*
- *That my milk will be sufficient and plentiful and that there will be no latching problem and no breast infections.*

Did I see all the things on this list come to pass? Well, no, I didn't. However I choose to focus on what I did see answered. I had a quick labour, under three hours start to finish. I had no more false labours after I'd sent this email. I went into labour on my own. I had no grazes and only a little swelling. I pushed five times not ten! I had a home birth and didn't need to be admitted after labour. As far as I know my baby was not stressed, engaged properly and his levels did not need to be tested. He pooped as he came out, not while he was in! He fed better than well and I had excess milk and no problems. If you compare this success list with what I didn't get, the negative seems minor. I did experience pain and I did tear. It's eight to two. We seem to default to the negative and focus on that. Regardless of whether I did see the whole list fulfilled or not, next time I will pursue and overcome until my greatest disappointments become my biggest successes. In our weakness He is strong. I will not let my next pregnancy be determined by my last one.

4

Conception:

Naturally fruitful

Labour is the end of a journey that starts with conception. Before conception we need to be in a place of faith, a place of knowing what we can have and what we are going after. Just as we should prepare our body for pregnancy we should also prepare our spirit. Our wombs are protective cocoons for our babies, but our spirit also needs to be a spiritual cocoon for our baby and our seed of faith. We need to be in a place of faith before anything comes at us. Our guard needs to be in place before a baby starts to grow within us, like a protective barrier, our shield of faith needs to be up, before any symptoms kick in or people start making negative comments.

It is also at this point, prior to conception that we can speak in a healthy, happy pregnancy. We can speak to our babies before they are formed, (Jeremiah 1:5), God already knows them so you can join with Him in the reality of Heaven and speak over, not only your baby but your body. We co-create with Him, He knows our baby and their destiny. We align ourselves with Heaven and speak it out over our lives. Tell your hormones to get ready and work correctly, speak acceptance over the baby's arrival. Proclaim a pregnancy filled with honour, that this baby will respect your body, not kick too hard or be incompatible with the safe surrounding you create. Make a commitment to your baby to be a hospitable environment for them, to always speak life over them and to love them from the moment you know they are there. Make an agreement to work together throughout the nine months.

I have no personal experience with finding it hard, or not being able to conceive. My first pregnancy was welcomed but unplanned. We planned our second child and 'tried' for three months before I fell pregnant. I wanted a boy so we were trying only when I thought I was ovulating to increase our chances of having a boy! (I have no idea if this is scientific but thought we'd give the old wives tale a go! Apparently boy sperm swim faster than the girls and get to the egg quicker, so if you only try to conceive on the days you ovulate then it will more likely be a boy. The egg stays fertile for a few days after release so if you try for a baby prior to it's release, by the time the egg is ready for impregnation the girl sperm will be in the right place!) I invested in an ovulation kit and according to the kit I never ovulated in April! After that we spoke over mine, and my husband's body, that we would have a boy and then we stopped trying for one, and just tried to get pregnant!

Through the power of the cross Jesus made a way for us. He has made us co-heirs with Him (Romans 8:17). We are co-heirs with the creator. We therefore have the power to create. At the point of conception your child is marked with his or her personality and features, the mix of DNA determines their hair colour, gender and height. I believe it is possible to speak to your body prior to conception, to ask God and to see your desires come to pass. If you have always wanted a child with a certain gender or eye colour, then preconception is the time to ask. We spoke in the creation of a boy and our second child was indeed a boy. (Although his eyes are blue not green as I spoke in, but I'm still learning! However, he does have curls in his hair as I declared). Many of you may think that this is a step too far, that things like this should be down to God's desire, His sovereign will. But God tells us that He will give us the desire of *our* hearts (Psalm 20:4). I believe Christianity is about a partnership, God wanting us to be involved in the process of life not just silent bystanders of His unfolding sovereign will. Of course I believe that God is sovereign, but in His sovereignty He has decided to let us have a hand in choosing, and making our own destiny unfold. I don't think that God wanted to make robots when He created humankind. Right in the beginning He asked Adam to name the animals, (Genesis 2:19), He partnered with clay and later made us co-heirs with His son, this to me doesn't seem like He wants us to sit and watch Him work, but to get actively involved in our lives and creation. Does it matter what colour your baby's eyes are? No, but it's worth an ask if you dream of something specific, because He longs to fulfil our desires! The Bible tells us the earth groans for the sons of God to arise, (Romans 8:19), I believe there is a generation of people rising up that will understand the full extent of this Sonship. People who will search out His Word, who will live out what they find there and do greater things than Christ (John 14:12). We are no longer slaves, but friends of God (John 15:14-16). We did not serve Him through slavish obligation; yes, He is still our Lord and master, but we are also Sons and co-heirs with Jesus. We have a high calling (Philippians 3:14), and a high position in Christ: we are kings in the greatest of Kingdoms (Revelations 5:10). As we realise our sonship we approach God in a whole different light. If we do not understand our position as sons, and we only act as slaves we view life from a poverty mentality, we don't take ownership over life and the earth because slaves don't have property. A slave would not consider that asking for a certain eye colour was even in the realm of possibility. Although some of what I suggest may be hard to swallow, my aim is to awaken you to an understanding of the limitlessness of our creative ability: to challenge perhaps some perceptions so that you can then make up your own mind on where you stand. A lot of what I will share I do so to provoke thought.

God wants to partner with you, so what do you want?

We are Sons and coheirs with Jesus

How much do you live in the reality of your sonship? How finished do you actively believe the cross made things? How sure is your faith in what He has won? Could you sleep in the midst of a storm like Jesus did? Whatever your circumstances, whether it's a storm of IVF, or doctor diagnosis, can you settle in a place of inner peace and rest knowing what the outcome will be because of the position you have? We know our outcome when we know His will. We can see His will because we know what His finished work on the cross achieved. Jesus knew in the midst of a storm that the boat would make it to the other side, He could rest, asleep, until the outcome He knew became reality. It was only because the disciples woke Jesus that He stilled the storm. I believe He only did so for their benefit. He would have slept happily through the storm to the other side, knowing He would arrive safely because He knew the will of the Father (John 5:19). Because of this I think that it is not so much about stilling the storms in our lives, but living peacefully in spite of them. Of sleeping through them or ignoring them if you will, because we are so assured of the outcome, because we have faith that comes from knowing Father's will for us to cross over. However, we are also called to still storms, I believe another reason that Jesus was sleeping was because He was expecting His disciples to calm the storm themselves. When His disciples woke Jesus He did not rebuke them saying 'just endure' because they would reach the other side safely: He did still the storm. We have the authority to still the stormy circumstances of our lives, but the key is to be able to draw on the inner peace that comes from knowing His will, and therefore our outcome. We rise up in peace when the storm comes and are able to stay in that peace until the waves calm. When we know the promises of God we can action them and wait patiently to see them at the same time, faith is active and we rest from a place of faith. Psalm 113:9 says "He settles the barren woman in her home as a happy mother of children." If your circumstance is finding it hard to conceive then you can pull on biblical promises such as these and know that this season of

Ask Holy Spirit to change any mindset you have that is slavish rather than a sonship mentality

barrenness has to end because He has promised you will be a happy mother. Then you can rest knowing that which is to come by faith.

I believe there is a tenacity to faith, a strength that is determined. "Faith is being SURE of what we hope for and CERTAIN of what we do not see" (Hebrew 11:1). If it is taking longer than you expected to conceive search the Bible and find what it says there about barrenness, (In the 'Scriptural Blueprints' chapter I have also highlighted some verses on conception). Before you start trying for a baby you can find in the first week of your journal information on what happens in your body in order to conceive. Take each step and speak to your body, command it to do what it needs to. We have the power to create with the words we speak (Proverbs 18:21), so by declaring and commanding over our bodies, things happen. Pray using the information and knowledge that you have. When you do, pray from a place of thanksgiving (Colossians 4:2), you know you can have children from the knowledge you have in His Word, thank Him for those promises. We can be thankful because we see what we can have in heavenly places, we know He has won access to those promises for us through the cross and we can have what is rightfully ours as sons of the King. When we pray we must also pray with faith, truly knowing the information that you pray will become reality because you have decreed it (Mark 11:24). The evidence of faith-filled prayer is thankfulness, because it shows that you know He has done it. Faith receives thankfully like receiving a gift; our gift is what He has already accomplished on the cross. A slave mentality would be waiting for God to do something, trying to twist His arm to hear you rather than sitting thankfully and expectantly for your inheritance as a son.

The key to faith is rest. In quietness and trust we find our strength (Isaiah 30:15). When a prince, or son of God commands his subjects to do the will of the King, he sits back and rests knowing that it will be done. He has faith in the authority of the King he is speaking on behalf of. So it is declaring the will of our King that enables us to rest. To declare God's will we need to know what His will is. We find out His will by spending time with Him and by seeing it in His Word. As we speak and pray the will of God over our body, our baby and our circumstances, we rest knowing the King's authority from which we speak. His words do not go unfulfilled (Isaiah 55:11); It's quiet assurance.

After my three months of "Am I pregnant...No." I can only imagine the depth of emotion that comes with repeated disappointment. I take my hat off to those of you who through disappointment continue to try for a baby. You are very brave and courageous. My words to you are, do not give up hope. When we find it hard to conceive, it is in the midst of great sorrow that He leads us into green pastures and makes us lay down (Psalm 23). Verse four of this chapter gives us a key; we are to 'fear no evil'. Fear is the enemy to faith because it makes us focus on the lack of possibility in our circumstances rather than the author of faith, the one who can do the impossible: Jesus. In Jesus not only do we find faith but rest. Matthew 11:28-30 says that He gives us rest in our souls, He exchanges our heavy burden for His rest in the work we have to do. Toil and striving for things were a result of the fall and Jesus has redeemed us from that curse. We were created to work from a place of rest. We can rest now in the good of what He has done, Jesus achieved it all on the cross, so we can enter His rest of faith. The only thing we need to strive to do in the Kingdom is to enter into the finished work of His cross! It all comes from knowing what He has done, not what we have to do. It is the rest of faith deep within our souls. Be at peace and prosper in your body even as your soul prospers (3 John 1:2). If your soul is in anguish your body is not at peace. When we know the position we have as a son, made available to us by the cross, we have peace because we know the family we are a part of, we know what is rightfully ours because of what He won. When we know what we can have, be it healthy bodies or conceiving easily, we are then able to get into a place of faith. The Bible is clear that we can have children if we

Rest in His very great goodness

We need to be sure and certain of who God is and what He wants for us, then from that assurance we are at rest

want them, that they are a blessing and that He wants to bless us. We can have them because we are a blessed people and out of that blessing flows fruitfulness (Psalm 127:3-5). None should be barren among us. (Exodus 23:26). God's design from the beginning was for couples to procreate; it is a basic human function; it is our right as women. If our soul prospering affects our bodies then we need to be well in our soul, and to be well we need to be happy. In His joy we find our strength. It has been researched and proven, both scientifically and medically, that if women are more at rest and happy they find it easier to conceive. This is also true for men. If men are stressed then they have a lower sperm count therefore making it harder to conceive.

We need to be sure and certain of who God is and what He wants for us, then from that assurance we are at rest. Do you believe that God wants you to have a baby? Do you believe that God wants you to have a baby now? Do you believe that God can heal you, and your husband, to make it physically possible for you to do so? These are all questions that you need to be sure of so that a tenacity can rise up on the inside of you that says, "I know my God and the plans He has for me. I will pursue until I see." In joy you find strength to keep trying because you know that God is for you. If He is for you then who can be against you?

◆

Philippa-Jo C Dobson

5

Our little secret:

In quietness and trust

People have very varying reactions to the "I'm pregnant" announcement. Mostly, people smile and hug, start to plan for the coming months by giving advice and words of experience. During my pregnancies, underneath all the seemingly friendly exterior I found something more sinister; negativity. In my first pregnancy, the first person my husband and I told was our doctor. The atmosphere in her office wasn't pleasant, perhaps she was having a bad day. For this I am now glad! Because of her blatant disregard for the new life inside me, it opened our eyes to how much of an affect the words of others can have a hold on our lives if we let them.

After I explained to the doctor that the home pregnancy test was positive, she looked sternly across to my husband and said, "I presume then, as you're here, that this is good news?" A little taken aback we nodded and smiled and she moved on. Tutting that I was not taking vitamins, (I didn't know I should be!) She wrote a quick prescription and handed us an appointment letter for a few weeks time. "This is your booking letter for the local hospital. Take this letter with you in a few weeks if the pregnancy lasts that long." She congratulated us then showed us to the door. We both felt a little deflated but decided that from then on we were not going to let negativity steal our joy; or let her negative atmosphere overshadow us.

Have you ever listened to the comments that come when someone announces they are pregnant? Let me give you some examples. "It's all sleepless nights from here." "Has the morning sickness kicked in yet? Ginger biscuits are good for that." "You'll feel better after your twelfth week." "Our fingers are crossed for you up through your first trimester." "Oh honey that's wonderful, and don't worry, the pain isn't as bad as you'd think." "Are you having a home birth? Good. I was at the hospital and it's so filthy you don't want a new born in that environment." "You're not having a *home birth* are you? That's not very wise for your first baby you know." I could continue! Most of these comments, and others like them, come from people wanting to help, to steer you away from the bad things they themselves have experienced. They are usually well meaning and I believe their aim is honestly to encourage you. But when you break it down like this, it doesn't feel encouraging does it? Some of the advice is helpful, however a lot of the advice on childbearing found in books, through friends and on television and websites, is often clouded with a negative slant. As we fill ourselves with the Word of God and become better acquainted with His truth, we also become more discerning; and we are able to 'eat the meat of what people say but spit out the bones' (John Wimber). Not all advice is digestible.

These comments will come regardless of what you say, but my aim for you is to be wise about who you tell what you are believing for. If someone is generally negative about pregnancy it is easier to rebuff, rather than take it as a direct attack on what you're believing you can have. For example, a small child is at school, bragging that her Daddy said she could have a pony for Christmas. Another child from a less wealthy family doesn't think that any father would buy a *real* pony for a child and says so. The teacher overhears the conversation and wondering if it was the child's wish, rather than the father's pleasure says, "It would be lovely if everyone's Daddy could buy a pony for them, but ponies are very expensive. Perhaps he meant he was going to buy you a rocking horse. They're a lot of fun aren't they?" The second child agrees, but the conversation leaves the first child deflated and doubting what her father had said. The teacher's aim was to save the child future heartache when they didn't receive a real pony for Christmas, and to not let wealth divide the children. What you can have all comes from knowing your father. If you know your father can afford a real pony then you won't settle for thinking that a rocking horse will do and if that child had not told of what they were believing for, they would have protected their hope. In the same way, all that is available to us comes out of knowing our heavenly Father and knowing who to tell about that relationship.

If someone says something general to you like "labour is painful, poor you, but don't worry you soon forget it." You can smile and let it slide off your shield of faith. However if you have told someone you are in belief for no pain in labour and they say, "I don't believe you can ask for that. And even if you ask for it, God doesn't always do it," your faith is more at risk of rocking because they are personalising, going to the heart of your faith and seeking to undermine it, even if unintentionally.

God's Word tells us that to have faith is to be sure of the things we hope for, and certain of the things we cannot see (Hebrews 11:1). If the words that others speak over us are negative, then it can rock our certainty and therefore our faith. Words carry the power of life and death (Proverbs 18:21), if people are speaking negativity over you it can literally come about, bringing death to your promise if you are not guarded by faith. Negative words are all too easy to speak and confessions that we make over ourselves are easy to accept as normal, but we need to examine our hearts and look at where the negative words are coming from. Matthew 15:18 says, "but whatever comes out of the mouth comes from the heart." Examine your heart; could it be fear of disappointment that leads us to say or accept statements about the negative aspects of pregnancy? It is very important to choose carefully who we tell what we are believing for. For many women, childbirth is often a very delicate subject. We all know many people who have had a baby, and each of these people have a personal experience of what you are now going through. If you make it known that you believe a pain-free labour is possible, then women who have had a bad experience often feel offended by your faith. Instead of laying aside their own experience and joining in faith with you, the response is often to try to give you a *'realistic'* view from their own experience. They are challenged by your high standard and try to lower it to their own standard of experience. I am sure this is not a malicious attack, but a well meaning 'reality check.' Their aim is to save you from disappointment by not letting your hope get too high. But it is clear that most of these well meaning words of advice are rooted in fear of failure and therefore unbelief.

Because the supernatural standard of childbirth is not often pursued it is difficult to find people who will rally around you and talk from positive experience. So whom then do you tell? If you have no one around you that you think will be a support in this area then you don't have to tell anyone, not even your husband if he is likely to be unsupportive. You and Jesus are enough. When people give you negative comments you can reply pleasantly, but it is not required of you to defend your position of faith by telling them you are expecting painless contractions.

Your faith is like a seed; protect it as you would in a natural environment, away from the elements of severe weather. It is difficult to grow your seed if it is continually being knocked down by other people, you end up fighting to keep them off rather than concentrating on growing your faith. Jesus promised us that even with faith as small as a mustard seed we could move mountains (Matthew 17:20). Ideally you want your faith to grow away from the negative elements, within the safety and nurture of a greenhouse environment. I hope you are able to find a group of friends to create that greenhouse effect, people who will surround you with positivity. I had six women (and my husband), I chose them because they are all women of faith, none of them had had great childbirth experiences, some of them didn't have children. I knew them all to be believers of the Word, people of prayer and some of them to have honed prophetic gifting. I gave these woman my 'I am believing for' list and they stood with me for what I was believing for. Some of them would give their opinions, but they did not expect me to always listen and do what they thought was best. They would challenge me on decisions and re-align my focus when I lost sight of what God had promised me. They became my greenhouse. Not everything they said was helpful, but in the main they protected my seed of faith. In the end it is your relationship with Jesus that gets you through, however a little help from your friends is a great support! Our greenhouse for faith can be erected at any point during pregnancy, it is never too late to start believing for a heavenly standard. However, the ideal is to have your shield of faith up, even prior to conception, so that your baby is born into a safe environment.

Not only do we want our faith to be protected but we want to protect *The Faith*. If we go into our midwife appointments mouthing off about how faithful God is, and how we aren't going to have drugs because we're not having pain, we will come off looking like religious quacks. If at the birth a complication arises that you were not prepared for and you end up needing drugs, because of your previous comments in the midwife's office God looks like the bad guy as most of the world don't have the view that God is good. The midwife has a negative experience of Christianity and it is generally a bad witness. However if when talking to your midwife she asks you what pain relief you would like. you can say, "Actually, I am hoping to do this naturally." This hasn't undermined your faith because you are sure of what you hope for, a natural birth. It also hasn't alienated your midwife to you. You come across as confident and sensible. If at childbirth all goes well, afterwards is the time to give testimony as to why. God then looks amazing, as He is!

You can choose to tell everyone you meet that God wants women to have babies with the standard of Heaven. It needs to be said, our culture needs to shift and Christians are the ones to do that. If you are able to stand firm in your faith then certainly tell the world, but I think wisdom says be wise in whom you tell when you are pregnant, not through fear but through protection of your faith. Leave the shouting from the rooftops until after you have finished this race. Isaiah 30:15 says, 'in quietness and trust is our strength.' When you do have a testimony it is then that others around you will be inspired to pursue God for the same breakthrough you have just accomplished.

I was planning on keeping my faith journey to my select few friends in my first pregnancy, but my husband told everyone what we were standing for. Remember the little girl whose father promised her a pony? When the teacher intending to do good shot her down, she could have politely told the teacher that her father was the richest man in the world, that all her siblings had ponies and now was her turn to get one. She could have said that the stable was ready and the pony was ordered, she had the receipt. As long as you can come from that kind of assurance when telling people what you can have in pregnancy and labour, then go for it.

How confident do you feel in what you are believing for?

If you are sure of what you can have, then you can tell people. If you know your Father then you can tell people of His character. During my first pregnancy, I found myself using phrases such as, "I'm very calm about giving birth; I'm choosing not to be fearful; I believe it is going to be an enjoyable experience because I believe that's the way God intended it to be." I know people were intrigued by how calm and relaxed I was about it all and even if inside they were thinking, "Just wait until she actually experiences it!" I know that I was reflecting the peace and security that I have in God. When the rubber hits the road, it is your own faith and relationship with Jesus that will lead you to receive what you are seeking in childbirth, and reflect it to the people you come in contact with.

✦

6

Think happy thoughts:

Joyful mother of children

It is a privilege to be a woman and have life grow on the inside of you, it creates that happy glow. Even in my first pregnancy, when I was sick all the time and felt the furthest thing from attractive, so many people would say how radiant I looked. I was glowing. At the time I thought it must be the lights reflecting off my sickly pallor! Now I think that there is an inner beauty, a joy that radiates through our faces, and I wonder if this is a small reflection of the Fathers glory, that emanated from His expression when He created the world. Pregnancy is about partnering with God in creating life and that is a joyous thing.

The challenge is to maintain joy regardless of how we feel, that our inner joy will then dictate to our bodies. 3 John 1:2 says, "Dear friend, I pray that you may enjoy good health and that all may go well with you, even as your soul is getting along well." There is a connection between our soul, our feelings and thoughts, and being in good health in our bodies. If we are not in 'good health' then I don't think we can experience the fullness of a heavenly childbirth, because we are more focused on the natural reality of our circumstances. A joyful soul is well, and lets us enjoy good health in our bodies. Our inner, healthy soul dictates that we have a healthy body. It is our inner monologue that will ultimately show and reflect to those around us. If we are confessing or thinking every day, "I feel so sick all the time" what are we expecting, - health? The Bible tells us that out of the overflow of our heart, what we feel and think, the mouth speaks (Luke 6:45). What I am not saying is that we should deny how we do feel. Throwing up then saying, "No, I'm not sick" is not faith. Can you see the difference in telling the truth and negative confession? Truth says, "I feel sick right now, but I will not stay in a place of sickness." Negative confession says, "I feel so sick all the time." You speak over yourself that tomorrow you expect the same thing, and you lose your hope and joy. You rob yourself of faith because faith is the substance of things hoped for (Hebrew 11:1) and you lose strength - joy maintains our strength (Nehemiah 8:10) all through negative expectation. ....

It can be a hard journey, I struggled with morning sickness for seven months of my first pregnancy, it was easier to give into sickness, to curl up and enjoy feeling sorry for myself. As in 3 John 1:2, the key to good health and things going well with us is keeping our soul well. A healthy soul is happy, content and strong. We are made up of three parts: body, soul and spirit, all equally important. Before we know God, we are primarily led by our soul,

What is your inner voice saying to you on a regular basis?

made up of our mind, emotions and will. When we are saved the Holy Spirit comes and dwells in our spirit man and becomes our leading motivation. Many Christians deny their soul, quenching their emotions, burying what they feel to obey God's Word without it touching their hearts. God wants our souls well, not buried. We are all an accumulation of our past experiences, upbringing and culture, expressed through our individual personalities. We are made unique and that diversity should be applauded, not stifled. To reach the fullness of a supernatural life, which is

We need to live as whole people, body, soul and spirit

Christianity, we need to live as whole people; body, soul and spirit. Jesus came to give us fullness of life. If we ignore our souls by not processing emotion correctly, if we suppress our feelings we are not living as whole people. I am not suggesting that we should all wear our hearts on our sleeves but certainly in British culture we have been taught to hide our negative emotional reactions. The effect is a little like taking an anti-depressant, we even-keel out. In the pursuit of hiding our lows, our highs have been knocked down too, rendering us as steady and some what dulled to life's adventure. To live supernaturally we must begin to learn what it looks and feels like to live naturally as God intended. As we are, the church as a whole is also made up of it's past experiences, cultures and revelations. Years ago a train of thought entered church culture; a view was formed that all natural things were not Godly and that only spiritual things were pleasing to God - this way of thinking was called Gnosticism. Much of the church, and us as individuals as part of it, still live with this warped view of Christianity. A lot of us believe that it is more holy or spiritual to go to a prayer meeting than to stay home and weed the garden. It is because we believe that our spirits are more holy than our souls that we push our emotions below the surface, hidden from the world and often ourselves. I believe our unwillingness to live as whole people is partly the reason why sickness is so rife in the church today. If we were to address our souls, to deal with our past experiences and process the painful, wounded areas we find there, our souls would be getting along well. We could then truly live from a place of inner joy and therefore have a healthy body. When things have wounded us, for example if someone has a father who is away for work a lot of the time, the child becomes hurt that Daddy was never there for school plays or football games. This child could then grow up to be an adult, still believing "I am not important enough to spend time with," or "Father God has no time for me just like Dad didn't." We need to deal with things that wound us by learning to keep short accounts. Through extending forgiveness to the people who have wounded us we keep our souls well. Without keeping these short accounts, offence leaves the wound open and it works it's affects into our day to day views. Something that could have been dealt with quickly becomes a paradigm that we view life through. If the child's parents had worked through forgiveness issues with the child early on, then they would not have grown up believing that they were not good enough to spend time with. A paradigm of unworthiness would not have been what they went on to view life circumstances through; their soul would have been healthy without this warped view of who they are. We all have certain view points, or paradigms, that we work from. As I said earlier we are all made up from the accumulation of the circumstances we were born into and have lived through. In order to live healthily in our souls, we must address the wounds that are still at play there. I am not suggesting that you go through each memory and process every one. But we get to choose if we live out of our past, or pull on the goodness of what Christ has won and walk in the fullness of redemption. It all comes back to relationship with the Godhead. As we enter His

To live supernaturally we must begin to learn what it looks and feels like, to live naturally as God intended

presence, Holy Spirit is there to guide us into all truth (John 16:13). This is not only the truth of who He is but it is also the truth of who we are in Him. As we see His view of us, we can renew our minds into the same view. As we forgive Dad for never being at football games we can give our feelings of unworthiness to God and ask for Him to show us His truth. We exchange the lies we've been believing about ourselves, God, and the world, for His truth. Truth becomes reality to us and as this exchange takes place our soul becomes well. We are content in our inner man and healthy in our soul, it's out of a healthy soul that we maintain a healthy lifestyle. It's in this place of the Presence where we can let go and be ourselves, as we see Him we are transformed into His likeness (2 Corinthians 3:18). 'Though you have not seen Him, you love Him; and even though you do not see Him now, you believe in Him and are filled with an inexpressible and glorious joy, for you are receiving the end result of your faith, the salvation of your souls (1 Peter 1:8).' Our souls are saved as we believe and trust in Him. If our souls are saved then they are in good health and so are our bodies. The word translated sometimes as saved, or healed or delivered, is the Greek word, 'sozo'. It means we are whole people, body, soul and spirit. God is interested in our whole self being healthy and prospering. When we receive salvation it should mean the entire package, that we receive sozo, healing, deliverance and salvation for our whole being. But salvation is a process (Philippians 2:12), and it can take time for us to see Heaven's reality. Like a mirror, it shows us the standard of where we are living and the lies we are believing. As we get healing for our wounds and give God the lies in exchange for truth we work out our salvation.

Joy is our strength. Our inner core that holds us up. If we are not living in joy it is so easy to slump under the atmosphere of heaviness, depression and negativity that threaten, looming above us waiting to crush our spirits. We can let the past colour our future by not dealing with what life has dealt us. The Kingdom of Heaven is righteousness, peace and joy. If these three things are operating in our lives we have a strong core and can remain upright under any pressure that looms. Joy is not just a gift of God that we can receive from Him, but it is also a general state of happiness and pleasure that has great affect on our natural bodies. So the challenge then is to keep our joy, regardless of how we feel. To stay in joy we must push back into His presence to receive strength for our bodies from the realm of Heaven that is full of joy. Inner joy, found in His presence, can then dictate to our bodies. Proverbs tells us that a merry heart is good for the body (Proverbs 17:22). A joyful soul makes us well.

Practically we need to make sure we are watching funny movies, spending time with friends, reading jokes and laughing regularly each day. We are intended to be surrounded by joy.

How many times do you laugh a day?

The very atmosphere of Heaven is one of joy, the Kingdom of Heaven is righteousness, peace and joy in the Holy Spirit (Romans 14:17), we have the Holy Spirit as an access point into His presence, Holy Spirit is there to lead us into the Father's glory, (John 16:13-15). In His presence is fullness of joy (Psalms 16:11), as we access His presence by simply turning our thoughts towards Him, as we become aware of Him and create a lifestyle spent in His presence, not necessarily part of your life drawn aside, but your current life lived aware of Him surrounding you. As we live in His presence the joyful atmosphere of Heaven also surrounds us, we find strength in His joy (Nehemiah 8:10) and as our souls are glad, our body will follow in health and peace. The atmosphere of Heaven penetrates our life, the Kingdom invades our space and our culture shifts from gloom to glorious joy. As we approach Him, He exchanges our spirit of despair for a garment of praise and the oil of gladness or joy instead of mourning (Isaiah 61:3).

Joy changes our outer circumstances and makes us see things differently, just like the people in 2 Corinthians 8:2, "In the midst of a very severe trial, their overflowing joy and their extreme poverty welled up in rich generosity." Their joy overflowed and changed the external outcome. So how do we obtain this joy? Romans 15:13 says "May the God of hope fill you with all joy and peace as you trust in Him, so that you may overflow with hope by the power of the Holy Spirit." Trust is the key to getting joy and we can only trust Him when we know Him. Again it comes down to spending time in His presence, the place where we can renew our minds. Where He "bestows on them a crown of beauty instead of ashes, the oil of joy instead of mourning, and a garment of praise instead of a spirit of despair (Isaiah 61:3)."

Thankfulness keeps us in a positive mindset that enables joy to reign, keeping you healthy and strong. If we confess the Word, the promises of God, and are thankful for them because in Christ we have already received them, then joy remains. It is not a blind confession of thankfulness, but faith that rises up in us because faith comes by hearing the Word. Our circumstances are real but His Word has been placed above all things. As we confess the Word and align our minds to believe it, the Word of God creates a greater reality. As soon as we let that spirit of despair have access, we start a slippery slope into negative thought, as joy is no longer giving us strength. Our bodies weaken and our circumstances get worse, making us deepen into mourning for the loss of health. If we are able to throw off all that entangles us and run with perseverance (Hebrew 12:1-3), we will receive a tenacious joy that says that no one can take the spring out of our step, or the bounce out of our ball. If you are struggling with morning sickness, rather than confessing 'I'm not sick' in blind hope, when in fact the circumstances say you are being sick (Or have Gestation Diabetes, or back pain, etc.), you need to realign your mind. We have choices. Do we let the circumstances pull us under, and give into the sickness or diagnosis, or do we do what sometimes seems impossible? James 1:2 says, "Consider it pure joy, my brothers and sisters, whenever you face trials of many kinds." Abiding in Him brings a joy and peace that is supernatural and refreshing. The Kingdom is righteousness, peace and joy, joy is the very atmosphere of Heaven and as we access heavenly places we are changed by its

How can you stop yourself if you are on a slippery slope of negativity?

atmosphere. The one in Heaven laughs at the enemy's tactics (Psalms 2:4), He laughs at the bad. As we come into heavenly places let's mimic its activity, and laugh at what may be an impossible situation in front of us, we laugh because we know that we are about to see God do the impossible. We laugh at the enemy's ridiculous attempts to rock us from our firm foundation because we know that his attempts are futile.

✦

7

Living from Heaven:
His Kingdom on earth

Heaven is our superior reality. The Bible tells us our position in the Kingdom through what Christ has done, is seated right next to Him in heavenly places. This reality, this world if you will, should be where we map out what we believe. What you see in this realm is what you can have and experience on earth. Jesus taught us to pray, "your Kingdom come, your will be done, on earth as it is in Heaven (Matthew 6:10)." We must know this realm in order to live it on earth. These verses in Philippians 3:20-21 sum it up so eloquently, "But our citizenship is in Heaven. And we eagerly await a saviour from there, the Lord Jesus Christ, who, by the power that enables Him to bring everything under His control, will transform our lowly bodies so that they will be like His glorious body." As we spend time getting to know someone, we use our senses to gauge what they are like, we watch their movements and hear their varying tone of voice. We use elements of all our senses to get a full picture of what their personality is like. God has made our senses alive in Him so that we can use our senses in the spirit realm, we can hear God's voice, see in the spirit realm and taste, feel and smell what Heaven is like.

We have both natural and supernatural senses

If I said to you "close your eyes and picture a baby's pram" in your mind you would see an image of a pram. This is your mind's visual centre. Where you saw the pram, in your mind's eye, is also the place that God uses to speak to you. Just as when He speaks to us in the still small voice (1 Kings 19:12) and it sounds like our inner monologue or conscience, He uses our visual centre to show us things through our spiritual eyes. God talks to us in many ways. We often have a default favourite, or easiest way that we personally communicate with God. I 'see' a lot, but it is my mission to become aware of all of my spiritual senses when spending time in His presence. There are many accounts of people smelling things, like flowers in worship, or feeling warmth, hearing angels sing, or tasting honey, (taste and see that the Lord is good, Psalm 34:8, and your name is like honey on my lips, Psalm 119:103, I believe are speaking literally). This is all available to us in the realm in which we are now positioned as sons of God. For me this is fun Christianity, a real and tangible faith.

During contractions in my first labour in my mind I was repeating, "Jesus take me to Heaven," I knew its reality was a better one so I wanted to be there. After labour, while the midwife was giving me stitches because of a tear, Jesus answered my silent prayer and *took* me to Heaven. In the midst of being disappointed that I had torn in the first place, the prayer that I had repeated during contractions was answered. I was still aware of my earthly environment, but when I closed my eyes and focused on Him, Jesus became my reality. Through my imagination I saw myself in Heaven with Jesus. He took me by the hand and showed me Heaven's reaction to the birth of my daughter. After this vivid experience I knew that I would be able to enter into the same thing again. I have done so many times, at first I thought it must be my imagination putting life to scripture I knew. But Jesus told me that Heaven is a real place, and therefore I can actually go there: it's not a reality saved only for death! Hebrews 4:16, "Let us therefore come boldly to the throne of grace, that we may obtain mercy and find grace to help in time of need." At one time during contractions I said my repeated inward prayer out loud, the look on my husband's face was priceless, "Is it really that bad?" he said very compassionately, looking at a loss for what to do. He assumed that I was in so much pain that I was asking Jesus to take me to Heaven because I wanted to die! As we become willing to lay aside our preconceived views of God, to trust in His presence, to lean into Him, even as storms blow around us, we are elevated above the ground warfare to soar with Him. The key is to dwell in the secret place of the most high (Psalm 91).

I decided to test this with some friends. We arranged to all 'go to Heaven' and see if we could look for each other! At eight o'clock one evening in our separate houses we engaged our spiritual senses, we all had different experiences with Jesus in our sanctified imagination, but when we later conferred, we discovered we had each seen each other doing exactly what we thought we had been doing ourselves. In my imagination I was flying in Heaven's sky, when I looked for one of my friends I saw her sitting beneath a tree and I got a sense that she was pregnant. I text her after this experience and asked her if she was thinking of becoming pregnant, she was shocked, she was a few weeks pregnant already and had only told her husband! When she looked for me in her imagination, she said she found it hard to place me, "it was almost like you were swooping around the sky!" Which is exactly what I had been doing. From then on, I have chosen to believe my heavenly encounters. I may not understand them, and it is most certainly not *normal*, but I believe that God wants to communicate with us using all our senses, He has sanctified us, including our imaginations. Remember that I am out to challenge some thinking? If you want to experience the realms of Heaven the way I did this is how I do it:

Get comfortable, put on some instrumental or soft worship music and close your eyes. Let the peace of God wash over you. In your mind's eye, picture the throne of God and Jesus at His right hand. (Reading something Ezekiel 1, and Revelations 5, before you do this helps you put in details to what you are seeing because they talk about Heaven).

Ask one of the Godhead, whoever you connect with the most, to show you something. For example. "Jesus show me where you have prepared a place for me (John 14:2-3)." Or "Holy Spirit, show me the storehouse of Heaven," (Deuteronomy 28:12 and Ephesians

3:16). Or "Father can I come and sit on your lap?" "Show me somewhere special." "Please take me to the crystal sea," (Revelations 4:6). "Show me what I look like in Heaven." "Jesus what do you think about me?" Anything you can think to ask is okay, it's a relationship.

Now wait and watch. Let your imagination take over and 'see' yourself being shown around Heaven. It may feel a little strange at first just as it is when we first start to communicate with God when we are newly saved. That's okay, discovery and learning are safe places. It may take a little time to get used to this new form of communication. Let all your senses become tuned to the spirit realm, you may 'hear' God speak or hear angels singing, you may 'smell' or taste something, you may experience something physical like heat or tingling, the aim is to become more aware of Heaven's reality and to create a deepened relationship with the Godhead.

After your encounter has finished write down what you have seen. Sometimes things I have seen in Heaven are a little outside my paradigm! If you don't understand something you have seen, ask. Ask God "what did that mean?" or "show me the premise for this in the Bible." He will never go against His Word, so this is our guide.

There are examples in the Bible of different people 'going to Heaven' or having visions, encounters or experiences. When Stephen was being stoned he looked and saw Jesus in Heaven, he became more aware of what was going on in Heaven, so much so that he asked Jesus to forgive his killers. He was so at peace in this superior reality of Heaven that he fell asleep (Acts 7:60). Do you want to know the reality of Heaven in your labour? You must practice being in the presence so that it comes naturally to you in a time of need. So that even if in labour your circumstances are against you, you can rise above them and encounter heavenly realms. In Daniel when he was having visions it often says, he looked, or he kept looking (Daniel 7). The key is to look and find, to keep looking until you find, and to look again if you didn't understand the first time. If I can leave you with one principle from reading this book it would be this; to maintain your focus on the reality of His presence, then whatever circumstances arise, you can rest.

To live Heaven on earth we need to understand the reality of that Kingdom, one way to do this is through our senses and in doing so we experience His Kingdom. But we also have the Bible that enables us to see what the Kingdom of Heaven is like. The Kingdom is one of the main things that Jesus talked about while on the earth. As we read about the Kingdom and confess its reality into our lives, we see the Kingdom come, on earth as it is in Heaven.

Are you familiar with what Heaven is like?

Confession of the Word is a powerful tool. Faith comes from hearing the Word of God. Speak the Word out loud, over your body so that your ears can hear it. God's Word is powerful, scripture is not simply words on a page that hold great meaning. The scriptures are living and active, (Hebrew 4:12), they are God's words and are very much alive. As you speak His Word over yourself and your baby, your circumstances then change to come in line with the words you speak. God said He will not let His words return to Him void but accomplish everything that He sent them to do (Isaiah 55:11). His word holds power and is life to you. We are to eat the Word, digest it into ourselves so that it can change us from the inside out. What we feed ourselves on is what we become. All scripture is God breathed, just as God breathed life into Adam. As we speak His Word, His breath breathes life over what we speak over in our circumstances. There is power in declaration, in speaking out loud. Not only does our faith rise as we hear the Word, but life is declared and goes out over our circumstances, I think it affirms what you believe in a completely different way than an internalised thoughtful prayer.

Scripture for me is where it all starts. The Bible is where you can find God's blueprint for life. Regardless of whether you experience God in your spiritual senses or not, we can take His words and hold onto them, we can action faith through the promises in the Bible alone. We have the choice to look at it or not. Blueprints are not just for looking at however, we can choose to build into our lives what we see there. We can see it in black and white and then erect it in our own lives in living colour.

Feed yourself on the Word. Read it, listen to it and confess it. I found post-it notes of scripture around my house made me read even if I wasn't thinking about it. On the bathroom mirror, by the kettle, wherever you are likely to see them frequently so that you digest little and often throughout your nine months of pregnancy.

Confession is not the only 'speech' tool we have. Commanding our bodies to function as they should makes a difference. We have been given authority, and as we speak our words create life. You are made up of three parts: body, soul and spirit. In chapter 6, *"Think happy thoughts: Joyful mother of children"* I have spoken about your soul prospering, I have spoken about fear and negative thoughts being a battle in your mind. Our bodies too have a part to play. All three of the parts we are made up of need to work in harmony with each other. Our minds need to confess over our bodies 'this is how it's going to work.' I found out what my body needed to do and spoke it over myself. Your circumstances have to line up with God's Word, because His Word is more powerful than any of our circumstances. Our babies also have to obey us. It's a commandment to honour your parents!
Read books, search the internet and find out what it is that your body, and baby has to do to give birth, then speak it over yourself. For example: "Body stretch where you need to stretch, baby get into the right position."

What does "on earth as it is in Heaven" look like? The more you live in the reality of Heaven through spending time in the Bible, through practising your spiritual senses and through spending time with God, the more of the reality of Heaven will transform your world. Through being in His presence your mind starts to renew, you start to think differently towards circumstances. You start to think of things from His perspective. The peace that comes from being with Him starts to linger around you, causing yourself and the people around you to be at peace. For example, when I was having stitches for my tear, I was able to find His peace and use my spiritual senses so that the reality of Heaven invaded my circumstances. Heaven came to earth as I attuned myself to become aware of it. As you cultivate His presence, you are able to live in another realm. Let's go after the more, living in awe of who He is, how big He is, and therefore how we can do the impossible because of His enormity. It all comes from rest, resting in the reality of Heaven and of who He is. If all things have been made available to us, then I choose to go after as much as I can, even when I don't have a full understanding. I want to live out of my depth, because then I know that God is huge, I can rest in knowing that He is bigger than my circumstances, I live wrecked by His awesomeness, by His overwhelming majesty by His amazing faithfulness and love for me. As I press into Him I can lean on the vastness of the creator of the heavens and earth, the powerful God of justice that won't allow the devil to trifle in my life. It's knowing Him that is the only way that this concept of a pain-free childbirth pulls off, it comes from a revelation of the Kingdom, and the King of that Kingdom. It's knowing Him that brings Heaven to Earth.

It's important to stay in a place of peace, resting in the goodness of God

✦

8

En Garde:

Guarding against negativity

2 Corinthians 10:5 "Casting down arguments and every high thing that exalts itself against the knowledge of God, bringing every thought into captivity to the obedience of Christ."

If a bad circumstance comes at us before we conceive, while we are pregnant, during labour, or after birth, we have the choice in our mind how to react. We can protect our truth, or we can choose to let our minds dwell on negativity. Eventually negativity will rob us of our faith. As negative thoughts enter our minds, we need to take them captive. Do not beat yourself up that the thought came, but tell the thought to leave and then proclaim the opposite over yourself. Remember, as we submit ourselves to God and resist the devil, he has to flee from us (James 4:7).

For example, if you think, "I will lose this baby, I have had some spot bleeding, that's not good," then stop, breathe. Dial down your anxiety level into the peace that is found in His presence. Proclaim

....

Remain

hopeful

....

the truth aloud, "Body you will not drop your fruit before it's time (Malachi 3:11). Jesus you said none should be barren among us (Exodus 23:26, Deuteronomy 7:1). Jesus you said you will complete the good work you have started in me (Philippians 1:6). Body, stop bleeding. Baby, I speak health over you. Cervix stay closed." Then go to the doctor and tell them about the bleeding and see a good report. Stay in faith not fear, continually press back into His peace if you feel fear.

Good things can be destroyed by the power of our minds. If you are happy and something bad happens, it is not the circumstances that rob you of your joy; it is because you have allowed your mind to be overtaken by the circumstances, and become unhappy. Fear robs us of faith.

For example, it is a bright sunny day and a girl is happily singing to herself as she skips down a street. Suddenly from out of nowhere a thief latches onto her bag as he runs past her, knocking her from her feet. Obviously she is stunned. Her elbow is grazed from her fall and she no longer has her bag. All manner of bad thoughts fill her head as she looks at the fleeing figure in the distance. Tears well up in her eyes as the emotion of the event controls her. It is at this point that she has a choice. Get bitter and curse the offender, or remain in a place of joy, acknowledging the emotions of violation but not being overwhelmed by them. What happened to her was awful, granted. However what if she reacted in the following way? As she stares, crying from the pavement at the fleeing thief, she hears the curses running round her head but smiles instead of vocalising them. "Bless you, with that money in my purse. May you be prospered in your finances, I prophecy an entrepreneurial spirit over you with the ability to make wealth. Jesus, find them and save them by your grace. I choose to forgive them." She looks down at her grazed arm, her heart is happy. "Holy Spirit, come restore me." She touches the blooded area and as she removes her hand the graze has vanished. She picks herself up, a little sad that she has lost her bag which has sentimental value, but continues on her way. She comes to a junction and feels a prompt to take a different path from her normal route home. Choosing to obey the prompting she feels from Holy Spirit to take a different path, as she turns she sees her bag strewn in the gutter. God has answered the desire of her heart and returned her cherished bag. Joy rises inside her and she overflows with thankfulness and adoration for a God who loves her.

When we choose to bless and not curse we align ourselves with the Kingdom of Heaven. We come in the opposite spirit to that which has attacked us. We stop the slippery slope that our negative thoughts want to take us down, and maintain our joy and happiness even in the midst of a bad circumstance. Romans 12:21 says, "that we are to overcome evil with good." I know that God responds to our joyous heart, our forgiveness and the grace and mercy we extend to others. He responds in blessing. When parents are proud of what their children have done they often respond by blessing them. God is no different, the bag was returned. It's a very different atmosphere than the one that would have occurred if she had let her negative thoughts, justified as they were, take over her mind. The atmosphere would have been gloom and despair. It may have even led her to question why God would allow such an act of violence towards her. This whole encounter comes back to the issue of sonship. When we know God as a good father we will never question His goodness. If we know we are kings then we react to this situation with authority to bless and to heal. A slave's mindset would look on this event with a 'poor me' attitude. The slave's bound mind would jump to thinking that *Think like* they deserved to be robbed, instead of being able, as a son, to decree a change of lifestyle over the thief. A son *a son of a* is able to speak healing over the graze; a son is able to listen to the prompting and be lead back to the missing *King* bag. The same circumstance has two very different outcomes depending on our lenses. Sonship or slavery. Romans 8:14 says "For as many as are led by the Spirit of God, these are sons of God."

When our lenses are changed from slave to son we then need to manage our hearts and minds. This rightful management will affect our outward situations. We have the choice to respond to negativity as the world does from a slave mentality, or to respond in the opposite spirit: one of sonship. Our words have the power of life and death, life to us and to those around us. Our words start as feelings in our hearts and then thoughts in our mind. What is on the inside of us comes out of us. What we harbour in our hearts ultimately comes out and either affects or infects the world around us. Our words are a powerful two edged sword (Hebrew 4:12). By the thoughts you think and the words you say you have the power over your outlook and your body. Proverbs 4:23 says, "above all else, guard your heart, for it is the wellspring of life". So it is at the point of thought that we need a filter on our minds. We need the grace to enable us to stop in our tracks and evaluate the thought and its source. We need to process our thinking and make a conscious decision to believe the right spirit. It comes back to being sure and certain of what God has told us. Sure of His words of truth. Sure of who He is, and sure of our position in Him. Remember faith is being sure of what we hope for and certain of what we do not see (Hebrews 11:1). We have to know exactly what we are believing so when negative thoughts come we do not doubt what we know to be true.

Study is one of the keys to success. Spending time with Him is another. We must be certain of the things we see in the Bible about childbirth, and certain of what we believe God has told us personally about our unique walk through childbearing.

2 Corinthians 10:5 was my challenge. "We demolish arguments and every pretension that sets itself up against the knowledge of God, and we take captive every thought to make it obedient to Christ." I had found the knowledge of God by searching His Word and seeking His face. One thing I found was that pain was not in His character to give, because by His character of love He took pain from us. I now had to guard this truth in my heart against my own thoughts and the negative words of others - be it friends or television. When I was pregnant and saw distressed births on television, portraying very painful labours, although they were often very comical scenes from films, they set thought processes off in my mind. I ended up avoiding these types of programmes during pregnancy, to protect my seed of faith. However it is harder to protect yourself from the random comments of others, unless you completely shut yourself off from the world! How can you live in the world but not conform to its pattern? (Romans 12:2). A pattern

that says labour is painful if you're lucky, but excruciating for most! It comes back to knowing that our position is living from heavenly places: a painless reality. If *I know* that truth for certain, if I know that through the cross Jesus took all my pain, when someone comes to me and says, "I was expecting no pain and I ended up having all the pain relief I could!" My mind has to filter the thoughts that this brings. The thought might come with a stab of fear "She was believing the same as me. I know she is a more spiritual person than me, why should I succeed if she failed?" The thought comes in a flash but the filter should automatically come back with "I am a different person, on my own journey. I know God's Word and I will see it. God is not a respecter of persons (Acts 10:34)." A tenacity replaces the fear and I am saved from the downward spiral of negative thoughts. I have renewed my mind to react from a heavenly perspective, one of sonship. Outwardly I smile, nod and sympathise with the woman telling me her story. The Bible tells us to mourn with those who mourn. I am genuinely sorry she did not see what she wanted. I empathise that she had pain, pain is never pleasant and I wouldn't wish it on anyone. I could choose to say something back to her negative jibe against me, but I do not need to defend myself. I know what I believe. Pain was her walk and that was very real for her, I do not want to come across as arrogant or pious. Often women feel like they have failed when they do not reach a goal such as pain-free labour. I do not want to belittle their experience. However the standard of Heaven remains the same, regardless of their experience. I do want them to be inspired to go after a pain-free labour the next time round. Having said that, if I cannot come across in love it is better to just mourn with them and determine in my heart that I will see the Word manifest in my journey of faith (Romans 12:15).

Determining the truth in our heart is an inner strength. We find that strength in knowing God. That knowledge helps us to combat negative thoughts. That inner strength is called faith. The certainty of the knowledge of God. We have to know the character of God to determine His heart on a matter. When I read scripture I try to find the theme of God's character running through it. For example, when people are trying to come at me with negativity about labour, the most common verse quoted to me is in Genesis where it says that because of the curse, God will increase the pain of childbirth. Implying that in the perfect conditions of a sinless Eden there was already a measure of pain to increase from. For me, looking at scripture trying to find the theme of God's character, I read it like this: If there was indeed a measure of pain in Eden, through Jesus we now live in a greater covenant than that of the Old Testament. God is in the business of redemption and He displayed this through the cross. Redemption always makes things better than they were before, because God only has us go from glory to glory (2 Corinthians 3:18). So I believe we can live above the perfect environment of Eden. Also through reading scripture to see God's character, I see a good and loving God. He is not out to hurt me in any way, not even to teach me something! I believe it is not in God's nature to invent pain. Even if it was in the garden pre-fall, then the Bible says Jesus took all our pain on the cross. So if we believe in the cross and that Jesus finished His work there, then all pain was taken, even the pain of childbirth. God's sovereignty is the excuse given many times for when people experience something that they do not understand, but God's sovereignty does not make Him double-minded; on the one hand taking pain on the cross but on the other giving it to us in childbirth. Prior to writing this book that reasoning was sufficient for me. However, this verse in Genesis is a huge stumbling block for many people so I have researched into its meaning and have detailed my findings in the next chapter, "Pain-free labour: Was that God's original design?" My thinking, leading up to my births were, "how would pain-free labour be possible for others if it was God's intention for us to experience pain?" Why work against God's will, claiming no pain when it's His 'will' and design for us to have it! But if it has worked for others then why can't it work for me?

Our shields need to be raised and ready to extinguish the words of others and the fiery darts of the enemy. It is knowledge in the character of God, in God himself, that we find strength. However the Bible tells us there is a rest to faith. It seems a strange combination, a shield of faith and a rest of faith.

Rest in the spirit, is something I don't think we know how to do very well. Even God rested to show its importance when creating the earth. At the beginning of everything it was essential to rest. If we were at the helm of the biggest endeavour of our life: if we knew the project would last for millions of years, would we rest seven days in? I don't think I would! Still if it is important to God then it should become important to us. It reminds me of the story in Luke, chapter seven, of the Roman solider who sent for Jesus when his servant was sick. He came to Jesus for Him to heal his servant, he told Jesus just to speak a word and they would be well because he understood authority. He understood that he didn't need to do anything, it was the words of Jesus that would battle for his servant's life. He could engage with God and then rest. Faith should not be a battle, but a quiet assurance of who you know. When your faith shield is up, it is not because you are about to run into a fray and be battered. The only thing that scripture tells us to strive for is to enter His rest. The most important thing is to be in His presence, which is rest. Hebrews 4:10-11, "For anyone who enters God's rest also rests from their works, just as God did from His. Let us, therefore, make every effort to enter that rest, so that no one will perish by following their example of disobedience". We can rest from our work, because we rest in His finished work. He has worked for us so that we can enter rest without working for it.

The only thing that scripture tells us to strive for is to enter His rest

If you are living in an impenetrable castle and a small frail man was throwing pebbles at your six foot thick walls of stone, I don't think you would be worried. You would rest and laugh at the man in his futile attempts to breach your wall. To sit and laugh you need to be certain and sure that your walls are thick and have a good foundation. Psalms 2:1-4 says "why do the nations conspire and the peoples plot in vain? The kings of the earth rise up and the rulers band together against the LORD and against His anointed, saying," let us break their chains and throw off their shackles." The One enthroned in Heaven laughs; the Lord scoffs at them."

I think we become far too aware of the enemy. We think that he is bigger than he is and don't realise that our shield is more like the walls of a castle. We must use our walls as a filter for the futile attempts of the enemy, who tries to send people to breathe negativity over us. Get peaceful about our position and tenacious that our walls are indeed thick. God is laughing at the enemy's attempts because they mean nothing! Find assurance in the fact that nothing is impossible for God (Luke 1:37), that God sits and makes a table for us in the midst of our enemies (Psalm 23:5). He shows the enemy that He is aligning with you then He sits, relaxes and eats as if nothing is the matter. Because nothing is the matter! He has conquered all and is already victorious. Let us really align with Heaven and laugh at the vain attempts of the enemy, laugh at the circumstances that try to rob us, laugh at negativity and feast with God in His presence (Psalm 2:4). My husband and I literally choose to laugh out loud when things go wrong, it can feel silly and put on, but the more we do it, the more heart-felt it becomes, until we are actually laughing, even if the laughing is only because of us knowing how silly laughing at nothing is! But after a few minutes we have a happy heart and have changed the atmosphere around us. I challenge you to give it a go!

In battle there are two stances, defensive and offensive. Both are needed to win. If you think of a fencing stance, and the French term 'En Garde,' the fighter is both relaxed and ready. They are defensive but also looking for the opportunity to attack. If in our spiritual walk all we do is defend ourselves from the devil, then we play a very one sided fight. It is good and right to defend ourselves, but there is also tenacity in the Kingdom. "The Kingdom of Heaven has been forcefully advancing, and forceful men lay hold of it (Matthew 11:12)." The Kingdom is one of offence; of moving forward; of demonstration. When a negative thought comes to you don't just take it captive, which is being defensive, but be offensive and proclaim the opposite, then the devil will give up because you're too powerful! We need to take up our place, our stance, armed and ready: castle walls firmly in place, with a horde of ammunition prayer, and scriptures waiting to be launched. We must be at rest, assured in our winning potential, ready to defend ourselves, but also to advance our territory and win! Why? Because Jesus has won the battle for us, when He died and rose again, He conquered all and finished the fight. He won every victory we would need to win, He did it on our behalf. The cross is not only a symbol but the turning point in the world's existence, it makes everything in Heaven available on earth today.

✦

9

Pain free labour:
God's original design?

We have discussed in previous chapters that Jesus took all our sickness on the cross; so we know we can live free from morning sickness and other pregnancy symptoms that make us feel lousy. We have seen that pain was also taken at the cross (Matthew 8:17). However, having no pain in labour is still a little sought after experience. For a lot of people it all comes down to the verse found in Genesis 3:16, "Unto the woman he said, I will greatly multiply thy sorrow and thy conception; in sorrow thou shalt bring forth children." Most Bible believing, supernaturally minded people don't have a problem praying and believing, for a healthy pregnancy, and possibly even an easy birth; but many cannot get past this verse to believe for a pain free delivery. They are happy to believe for no sickness or pain in other areas, but they firmly believe that pain was always God's intention for childbirth. The wording in this verse implies that if the curse increased pain, then there must have been at least a measure of pain to increase from prior to the curse. Although I was able to get past this verse when going after a pain-free labour for my own births, by believing that Jesus won for me a greater covenant than even original design, I found that a lot of people struggle with it. It became clear that if I was going to publish this book I would need an explanation of Genesis 3:16 if I wanted to challenge people's paradigms on birth. I think we need to go back and read the verse in Genesis without assuming we already know its meaning. I delved a little into the original text with an open mind to see what I would find there. Through this chapter I hope to make clear to you God's original design for childbearing. So can I ask you, just for a moment, to lay down any pre-conceived ideas and come with an open mind?

Jesus won for me a greater covenant than even original design

Everything comes down to knowing God and viewing this passage from Genesis is no different. When someone knows God as good, they understand that pain is not in His nature to give. Pain is a part of life on earth, but it is a signpost. If you put your hand too close to a fire it starts to hurt; if you're chopping up food, and your finger gets in the way, pain tells you that something is wrong. Pain is an indicator that tells you to come away from the fire or, you need to stop putting pressure on the knife! You may need to go to the doctor to check what is causing the pain, but pain is not the problem, it just points to the source of the problem. To have pain in labour, if there is nothing wrong with your body, is to say that your baby is the problem! Women's bodies were designed to bear children, it's a natural function and there is nothing wrong with your body when you give birth, so it should not need to use pain as a signal to tell you something is wrong. I am not saying that women will never experience pain. You may have pain if you develop a complication, because your body will be sensing that something needs to be fixed, for it to work as it's designed to. Pain is the indicator that there is trouble. It's widely believed that only humans experience pain during the birthing process, although for animals it is obviously an intense activity, it doesn't appear painful. The battlefield of the mind, I believe, is the reason for this difference between animals and humans giving birth. The birth process is a normal part of life, if you have no warped lenses, your mind knows it is normal and therefore your mind and body are relaxed. When your viewpoint

there is nothing wrong with your body when you give birth

on birth is compromised by lenses that say normal is, 'that you have no idea what may happen, excruciating pain could kick in at any minute,' fear of the unknown, and fear of pain, brings pain. When your body tenses and is no longer relaxed, you are unable to birth without pain. Your thought process and your expectation of possible pain have literally dictated that you will have pain. If faith is the substance of things hoped for, faith is a positive expectation, fear mirrors that, fear is a negative expectation - to be fearful is to have faith in failure. Satan has been out to keep women in bondage since the fall and has done a good job of it. Much of the world is coming into the understanding that women are an equal heir with Christ, just as men are, we are worth paying the same amount as men, and we should be allowed to vote! But I strongly believe that the mindset of sickness and pain filled childbearing is a huge stronghold that needs changing not only in the church, but in society. I believe it is one of the last things satan has keeping women bound. I believe that we will see a complete paradigm shift in the way that society views pregnancy and birth in the next few decades. Even in the world you can already see the beginning of this in the rise in popularity of natural techniques and Hypno-birth. Women are actively pursuing ways to obtain a more relaxed and pain-free experience; women who aren't even aware of Heaven's standard are having great pregnancies and pain-free labours. How much more should we, who know Heaven's King, be turning our attention not on a focal point like Hypno-birth but on our Saviour, the one who came and took all pain. I don't believe that if God intended that it was original design for women to experience pain, that any woman would be able to experience a pain-free delivery. Why would God allow us to go against His plan? The only thing that goes against the plan of God is the demonic, it's ridiculous to think that the demonic plan for women is to birth pain-free and God's plan for us

The mindset of sickness, and pain filled childbearing, is a huge stronghold that needs changing, not only in the church, but in society, I believe it's one of the last things satan has keeping women bound

is to be in pain! It's sad because when we boil down to it, that is what our warped lenses would have us believe. Shocking! Let us rip off this twisted thinking and go after a supernatural standard in birth. I have heard some woman say that having a pain-free labour is not that important to them. Although I agree that we should not be disillusioned if we do have pain, my attitude on this is "really?!" Why not believe for pain-free? Why not go after it? Why would you not want to? But that's just me! As I've said throughout this book, all these principles come from a place of knowing Him, in His presence. If you choose to push in and see what is available then you can have it. I prefer the pain-free option! If Father God is good, then just like natural fathers He does not want His children in pain. I believe a good Father God would not have designed pain in His original plan. When you know Father as good then you come into a greater revelation of what is available.

it's ridiculous to think that the demonic's plan for woman is to birth pain-free, and Gods plan for us is to be in pain!

1 Timothy 2:15 says, "But women will be saved through childbearing—if they continue in faith, love and holiness with propriety." The word saved encompasses the complete person, made up of our spirit, soul and body. Saved means to be made well in our whole person. Using the various word choices from the meaning of the original text, this verse could be translated as follows:

"A woman will be made well, healed, kept safe and sound throughout childbearing, if she remains faithful in a relationship of love with God, through consecration to Him, trusting in who He is with soundness of mind".

This is the very essence of pregnancy in His presence. To continue faithfully pressing into a love relationship with Him is where any hope of a pain-free labour is placed, a deep rooted trust in Him, as we renew our minds by spending time in His presence. We are saved through childbearing. In context this verse and the verses around it are directly referring to the fall, the point where pain became a reality in childbearing, and '*notwithstanding*,' (King James Version), women are now saved in childbearing. Regardless of the curse, regardless of original sin, regardless of whether you believe that pain was there prior to the fall, woman are now, in New Testament covenant, saved - spirit, soul and body, in childbearing.

I want you to have a look at Genesis 3:16 in different translations. I propose that it is the lenses of society, through history's experience at work, that we view this verse. I believe that the stronghold of belief that says pain in childbirth is normal, is prevalent in society, in our churches and in our minds; and it was even present when the Bible was translated into English. When you translate, there is a measure of interpretation that you have to do, in order to put the meaning of the original across in the most understandable way. Sometimes, there are multiple words to choose from when looking at the original language. Gods' Word is absolutely His sovereign Word, but we can often draw a deeper flavour of its meaning from reading more than one translation. Let's look at Genesis 3:16 in some of its forms and look at the original Hebrew. As we read, Holy Spirit is there to lead us into all truth:

New Living Translation: I will sharpen the pain of your pregnancy, and in pain you will give birth.

Old King James: I will greatly multiply thy sorrow and thy conception; in sorrow thou shalt bring forth children.

New International Version: I will make your pains in childbearing very severe; with painful labour you will give birth to children.

New International Version 1984: I will greatly increase your pains in childbearing; with pain you will give birth to children.

New American standard: I will greatly multiply your pain in childbirth, in pain you will bring forth children.

Amplified: I will greatly multiply your grief and your suffering in pregnancy and the pangs of childbearing; with spasms of distress you will bring forth children.

The Message: I'll multiply your pains in childbirth; you'll give birth to your babies in pain.

Good News Translation: I will increase your trouble in pregnancy and your pain in giving birth.

Although the varying translations of Genesis 3:16 are very similar, there are drastic differences, that if you were skim reading you could miss. Translating Genesis 3:16, in the very worst way it can possibly sound, it reads as follows;

"Greatly will I increase your pain in pregnancy, or conception; In pain you will birth children."

Even now it clearly does not say that any increase of pain will happen in labour, only in pregnancy or conception. This verse implies that if there was pain in original design, it was only in pregnancy or conception. Birthing or labouring in pain only came in with the curse. In Isaiah 53:4 it says, "Surely He has borne our griefs and carried our sorrows." Jesus took all this 'pain' on the cross, because He carried our sorrow, which means pain, both mental and physical. Regardless if pain was originally intended in pregnancy and labour or not, I believe that if Jesus carried our pain, it means *all* pain. Surely! No exceptions, regardless of His original design, He did not go against Himself but made us a better covenant.

Using the Old King James version (as this is what Strong's concordance uses) I will break down each section of Genesis 3:16 to look at all the varying ways it could be translated. Here is a reminder of the whole verse: *"I will greatly multiply thy sorrow and thy conception; in sorrow thou shalt bring forth children."*

"I will greatly multiply thy": *'greatly'* and *'multiply'* are the same word *'Rabah'*, it is this word alone that the argument for pain in original design hangs on. In Genesis 3:16, it is implied through the translating of the Hebrew word *'Rabah,'* as *'increase'* or *'multiply,'* that pain already existed prior to the fall. To increase something, a measure of that thing needs to be at play in order to increase from. If you multiply from zero, by any amount, you will always get an outcome of zero, for example 0x10=0; if however we put pre fall labour pain at a score of one, the curse comes and multiplies it, by let's say ten, then you have a sum of 1x10=10, an outcome of ten being a high pain score. So pain in childbearing with the curse is now at a ten, but Jesus came and redeemed us from the curse bringing the pain level back down to the pre curse score of one. People believe that we cannot labour pain-free because of this original pain level of one.   As sons of God, we are able to live in Heaven's standard, pulling Heaven's sickness and pain-free reality to earth, but people argue that there is no childbirth in Heaven, therefore the only standard we have to go by in childbearing is the standard of what we see laid out in the garden of Eden, a pre curse standard of a pain score of one; therefore they think that believing for pain free labour is not biblical. If the word *'multiply,'* or *'increase'* was not present in the wording of the curse, we could take it that there was no original pain in childbearing. If the wording of the curse made it clear that pain started at the pronouncement of the curse, rather than pain being increased from a small measure of pain to greater pain, then we could assume that it would be easy to place pain as part of the curse, and therefore taken away from us by Jesus on the cross. When I did a word study of *'rabah'* I was so excited by what I found after only a few minutes of searching! The word can be translated a few different ways: *"multiply,"* or *"be,"* *"become numerous"*, *"great"* or *"many."* If you replace *'increase,'* or *'multiply,'* with the alternative word of *'be,'* for example, that drastically changes the verse to read "Great will **be** your pain." That shows that there didn't have to be any measure of pain to increase from! Original design could just as likely have been NO PAIN! Translating of the word *Rabah* as *'be'* implies that pain only entered childbearing at the point of the curse, it was not in play prior to the fall. Jesus has redeemed us from the curse so pain-free childbearing is not only possible, but it is rightfully ours through what Jesus has done by taking all of our pain on the cross.

"Sorrow" is the next word in the verse. Isolating the word *sorrow*, `itstsabown`, you can see how sometimes it is translated *'pain'*, it can also mean, *mental or physical, pain or sorrow, hardship, labour or toil*. It is just as likely to mean that women will have increased mental pain, such as fear surrounding childbearing as it is to say that we will have increased physical pain.

"And thy conception", The word *'conception'* translated is *'Herown'*, and it only has two options for translation; *conception* or *pregnancy*. This word *herown*, in a few translations is translated as *'childbearing'*. Although conception and pregnancy are within childbearing, the word childbearing can be misinterpreted as only meaning childbirth, making us think only of labour. This word *herown*, is used only two more times in the Bible, and both times it's translated as *conception*, (Ruth 4:13 and Hosea 9:11). So any multiplying of pain is only in conception or pregnancy not labour.

When putting it all together the complete first half of the verse reads, *"I will greatly multiply thy sorrow and thy conception."* This is the only section of the verse that the word *'multiply'* could apply to. Following on from this, there is no indication in the remainder of the verse that pain was already present in the garden. The increase of *sorrow, pain, hardship* or *toil* is only relating to conception or pregnancy, not birth.

Now let's look at the remainder of Genesis 3:16, *"in sorrow thou shalt bring forth children"*.

"In sorrow" Sorrow or `etseb` is a different word than the previous word translated as sorrow. It can mean pain and in the main is translated as pain rather than sorrow. It could also mean, *hardship, labour, toil, hurt* and even *offence, vessel* or *idol*. When using the various translatable words, the meaning of the sentence is tweaked to imply slightly different things, *'In sorrow you shall bring forth* children,' or, 'In hardship you shall bring forth children,' or 'In labour you shall bring forth children.'

"Thou shall bring forth children" can be translated, 'beget children', (conceive), or birth.

From looking at the varying ways the original language of this verse can be translated, this is how I would personally translate Genesis 3:16:

"I will increase your toil in pregnancy and conception; in pain you will bring forth children."

In original design Adam was to work the garden, but work back then came from a place of rest. In the same way conceiving and carrying a child may have always been, 'work' but from this place of rest in His presence. The curse, I believe, increased this work into toil, making it hard work, without the place of rest in the garden. Now, through the cross Jesus has re-introduced this rest back into our lives, removing 'hard' and simply making pregnancy work, from a place of rest. Jesus has redeemed us from the curse so pain in bringing forth children is eradicated completely.

I do have one other thought on the translation of the verse: this is a little out there which is why I have chosen to add it at the end of this chapter. It uses the variable words and does not include pain at all in the curse:

"Great will be your sorrow in pregnancy and conception; in sorrow you will bring forth wickedly behaved children."

"Thou shall bring forth" can be translated, 'beget children', (conceive), birth, or it can imply, to bring forth wicked behaviour, if this is the case we can see that this curse indeed did come to pass, Eve's child, Cain, murdered Abel, and each subsequent generation has done wicked things. Adam and Eve did wrong, but wickedness is more than choosing to sin, it means evil or morally wrong. Eve would be robbed of the joy of birthing innocence into the world, her seed would now be tainted with the curse and she would be forever sorrowful of this.

My point is that we have assumed for too many years that the curse is full of pain. Not only that, but we are believing a good God would design pain as part of His plan. I hope that what I have laid out has challenged your viewpoint on this verse and made you even more hungry to know His character throughout His Word.

In the following table I have outlaid all the various possible word translations together from Strong's Concordance using the Old King James version of the Bible. Have a look and make up your own mind of how the verse could, or should, have been translated:

King James Version: "I will greatly multiply thy sorrow and thy conception; in sorrow thou shalt bring forth children."

OKJ original verse (read downwards)	Word choice substitutes	Strong's ref
I will		
Greatly multiply	*Be, enlarge, grow great, increase, make large, multiply, to make much to do, do much in respect of, transgress greatly, to shoot or become great, many, much or numerous*	7235 used for Greatly and Multiply
Thy		
Sorrow	*Pain, Labour, Hardship, Sorrow or Toil*	6093
And thy		
Conception	*Physical conception, Conception or Pregnancy*	2032
In		
Sorrow	*Pain, Hurt, Toil, Sorrow, Labour, Hardship, Offence, Vessel, Creation, Object or Idol*	6089
Thou shalt		
Bring forth	*To bear, Beget, Gender, Travail or Bring forth: childbirth, distress or wicked behaviour*	3205
Children		1121

10

The standard remains:
Don't believe a bad report

Family history

The first midwife appointment asks for your complete, negative and terrifying family history. I had no idea if anyone in my family had ever had a heart problem or polio. The things I could remember where horrific enough when you saw them all written down in one place! Fear then tries to take over, with thoughts such as, "what if the baby has x, y or z." As these fears drip into your thoughts, if you let them take root they will become a stumbling block. We are forced to look at the reality of our earthly situation and heritage. In my mind I did a quick stock check of every one of the things on the list that could be hereditary and sharply pulled in a breath. I had to stop my mind from continuing down the slippery slope I had started it on.

Where is our new position? Seated in heavenly places. There is no sickness in Heaven. We are co-heirs with Christ. We can access everything that Jesus did because He made a way for us. We are sons of God, grafted into His family (Romans 11:17). If God is my father then I can claim His heritage. I am in His lineage now, part of His royal bloodline. My inheritance in Him is health, the earthly hereditary line has been broken. No matter what my earthy inheritance could look like in the physical, I have now been made new. For me and my baby, we can live free because Jesus already paid.

Take the things on your family history list and confess health. For example, "I break the cycle of hereditary bad eye sight over my baby. I declare my baby has a new inheritance. Eyes, be well, function properly at one hundred percent vision. Baby, I speak over you that you will never need glasses. I break every curse on my family line that says this will keep happening and I draw a line in the sand using the blood of Jesus to say no more." We are a covering for our children, they are under our care while they are young, let's take up our parenting responsibility for them and stand in the gap of intercession on their behalf. "But as for me and my household, we will serve the LORD" (Joshua 24:15).

Down's syndrome and other disorders

During the first scan of my first pregnancy I knew that something was wrong. The expression on the Sonographers face was easy to read, although she said nothing so I left thinking that I must have read her wrong. The following morning I was on my way to work, I had forgotten to charge my phone and as it rang I debated whether to pick it up but I did. It was the sonographer from the scan. She assured me there was nothing to be concerned about but dread immediately crashed around me. My fears from the day before had been realised. She asked us to come in again after the weekend for an additional scan. She thought she had picked up a heightened nucal measurement (this is the measurement of the thickest part on the back of the baby's neck) and wanted a second opinion. If this was the case she would send us to the councillor for further arrangements and to talk through the possibility of our baby having Down's syndrome as any baby with a measurement over two millimetres are in a high risk category. I was so conscious that my mobile was about to expire, I thanked her and hung up. I rushed through Oxford Street to work and dissolved into tears as I tried to call my husband. He was going into a meeting and I was only able to tell him the few details I had before we hung up. My husband said one key thing "Remember we said we will not believe any more bad reports?" Our GP had been negative towards the news of my pregnancy right at the beginning. After the visit to her office we had decided that we would not believe any further negative words spoken over us. This helped. Although my emotions were still reeling, this statement provided me with the faith I needed and reminded me that God's plan for our baby was good. I was a mess and unsure of what to do. I couldn't return to my reception post looking like I did! I knew I needed support. I called a few select friends who I knew would pray and bolster my very tiny faith. They were amazing and I was able to compose myself. I still felt wobbly but I knew this diagnosis was a lie. Even if on Monday they told me that our baby had a problem medically, I knew that Heaven was free from sickness and it was therefore a lie. I was still upset but confident that God was for us. Faith is the title deed, the substance of things hoped for. A title deed proves that you own a property; you have proof of what is yours or what will be yours. When we know what is ours then we can be secure in an unflappable state of rest, so at ease and sure that there will be no other outcome.

However, the weekend was tough to get through. I knew that God would come through but grief and thoughts of doubt attacked my shield of faith. It was the unknowing that I hated. We prayed, we got prayer and we contended for a place of peace. We bound and loosed everything we could think of! Whilst praying one night I saw a mental picture of a small insignificant demonic creature squeal for its life and run far from us. It gave me the confidence that this was no big deal to God even though it felt like our whole world. We have authority to bind and loose, the devil has been defeated by Jesus and has no place to talk to us, or meddle in our lives. We can bind and rebuke him from messing in our affairs by taking hold of our authority and reminding him that he is defeated. The devil, his workers, pain and sickness, all have to leave when we command them to. They are no match for the authority in whose name we speak.

By Monday we were sure of God's plan. His will for all of us is health and wholeness. We prayed nothing missing, nothing lacking. It was time to go and get a good report from the doctors. On the way to the tube station we asked every person we walked past if they needed healing of any kind and offered prayer. If the devil thought he could mess with us then we were just going to release the opposite to what he was trying to put on us. Then he'd think twice before messing with us again! We sowed where we needed to reap, taking back what he was trying to steal from us. Think back to chapter 8 'En Garde' where we looked at how we are to be both defensive and offensive. Well, the devil is the same, he is on the offence looking to kill, steal and destroy, (John 10:10), but by actively standing in a place of faith we put him on the defence as we release the fullness of life that Jesus brings.

he'd think twice before messing with us again!

The second scan confirmed that we were in the high risk category for Down's syndrome or other chromosome disorders. They took us to see the councillor who had a box of tissues at the ready. We were not put off: in fact I was so pumped up I felt like I could take on any manner of attacks! I was sure that even though we now knew we were high risk , we would definitely have a testimony to tell from this. The councillor was really confused by our upbeat mood. My husband explained that God was keeping us calm. She changed tactics and said, "Some people wonder 'why them', 'why has God put this on us'." We smiled and shook our heads. We explained that God was in the business of blessing not cursing since Jesus had taken all God's wrath on the cross and therefore had none left for us! God wanted our baby well and that was what we were going to have. A healthy baby, with all its chromosomes intact. She was thoroughly confused now! She talked us through the medical facts and the options available to us. We opted to have a Chorionic Villus Sampling, or CVS test, that would give us a definite diagnosis. It was the not knowing that was driving me crazy. I knew that God would heal the baby if there was anything wrong but I didn't want to spend the remainder of the pregnancy on 'high alert faith'. When believing for something like this you have to keep up your guard. People around you will try and sympathise rather than stay in faith with you, you continually have to remind yourself that God can do it in order to strengthen yourself in the

Lord (1 Samuel 30:6). It's very easy to let moments of doubt become strongholds of unbelief. Personally it was an intense time of renewing my mind and taking every thought captive. I understood that I was in a moment of 'high alert faith', to battle the fiery darts of negativity. For me, faith at that level was fine for a couple of weeks, but I didn't feel like I could maintain it for the rest of my pregnancy. I wanted to strive to keep in the rest of faith. I also wanted to be armed with the information of how to pray. If the results were normal then I could move on, however if the results proved positive then I would know how and what to pray. For me, not knowing wouldn't enable me to stand on anything as I wasn't really certain if there was a problem or not. I wanted to know. I could have stood in faith for a healthy baby regardless of knowing the test results, I could have maintained rest, but the test was offered to me and I felt peaceful about choosing to have it.

Scripture says that Jesus is far above everything that can be named (Ephesians 1:20-21). To avoid possible bad news, by denying that anything is wrong is not applying the Word to the circumstance. When we pray we need to be specific, if you have a cold but keep saying through sneezing "I'm not sick," you are in denial, you need to face facts, "I'm sick". Then you need to go to the Word, find the truth and apply it to your cold, "I am made well by the power of the cross. Body, come in line with your new inheritance of health". So if Jesus is above all that can be named then we need to name it, sickness, Down's syndrome, or whatever else that is not lining up, we need to not be scared of the truth, of our bad circumstance or diagnosis, but know that The truth, (remember that truth is a person, Jesus), is above all things, that truth overcomes (John 16:23), truth sets us free (John 8:34).

The CVS procedure was painful but quick. Using ultrasound for visibility, a long needle is inserted into the womb, through the mother's stomach and a small amount of amniotic fluid is collected then sent for testing. The first set of results would take three days to come through, followed by the second set, ten days later. The battle to stay in faith was very intense and I was grateful that we had a Church conference titled 'Faith' on at the time so I was able to immerse myself in God's presence each night. That was my key. His reality had to be more real to me than my own. It was an emotional roller-coaster between tears and peace. It was in times spent in worship, in the heart of His presence that peace washed over me. We sought the Lord for His perspective and were given many encouraging words. For example, the fact that Jesus changed the molecular structure of water to transform it into wine encouraged me the most. God was in the business of changing scientific fact. His sovereignty can do all kinds of crazy things for our good! You see, it is as we spend time in the reality of Heaven, as we are immersed in His presence, as we lean on His sovereignty, the anointing breaks the yoke (Isaiah 10:27). It is intimacy with God that is the source of supernatural power. Attune yourself to become aware of our omnipresent God and let the reality of His Kingdom wash over you.

The test came back negative, and we were able to find out that we were having a baby girl! I was so overwhelmed by God's faithfulness, I cried all the more! We then told some of our family what we had walked through and the response was still negative, "What ever happens we will still love the baby when it's born." That was great but it still proved that even when God does something amazing sometimes we are the only ones to acknowledge it. And for some, even with the knowledge of medical fact, negativity is still their default setting. I believe that God healed our baby.

Gestation Diabetes

Throughout pregnancy woman are tested for all kinds of conditions. It is wonderful how modern medicine can test us and find out what our bodies and babies are doing, this has helped and saved many women and their babies. Having information, even negative, gives us a focus in prayer. If we know medically something is wrong, we can then pray to see that condition changed through the power of God.

Halfway through my second pregnancy I was tested and diagnosed with Gestational Diabetes. At first I was so irritated with not being able to just have a 'normal pregnancy' it felt like I was contending for everything! I really struggled that first day to stay on top of my emotions and frustrations. I had to find a place of peace. I told myself that I would grapple with the why later and for now accept that this was my circumstance, Diabetes. Now, what was I going to do about it? I would sleep through the storm. I told my body enough was enough and spoke to my insulin to function properly. My husband prayed with me but I was still feeling emotional and unsure about what would happen. I knew that God would sort out the levels but I was anxious for the circumstances in which my baby boy would be born. I wanted another home birth. The hospital however had me in the high risk category because of the Diabetes and I was therefore told that a home birth was not an option. Lots of negative things were said over and about me and my unborn baby. At first I was upset but then I remembered what God had told me. When I was praying, before my diagnosis, about whether or not to book a home birth (we were in the process of buying a house and I wasn't sure where we would be living and if it would be suitable), I felt Holy Spirit tell me that "You will have your home birth and your labour will be quicker than last time."

Having God's insight on the situation, I spoke over my body again. If God had said I would have a home birth that meant that I was not high risk. I didn't want to put myself or my baby in any danger but I knew that God would also not say something that would prove to be dangerous. I took what God had originally told me back to Him. I wanted to see if it still stood as my circumstances had changed. His answer was yes, and my faith was boosted. I was now in faith and sure of the outcome. In Heaven the reality is no Diabetes so the reality had to manifest here on earth. If my body came up to Heaven's standard then the medical staff would have no reason to deny my home birth. My levels went back to normal with an occasional spike from time to time. I would apply the Word again and the levels quickly came down until they were consistently normal.

Being 'high risk' I had many more appointments than in normal pregnancy, at each appointment my husband and I quietly explained that we understood the medical staffs concern for me having a home birth; we weren't anti-hospitals but that I wanted to be at home. I was reasonable, I explained that if my levels were high enough to have to go on insulin, or consistently spiking, if the baby was in distress, or had too much amniotic fluid then I would do as they asked and have a hospital birth. I was happy to admit that if my faith did not work then it would be dangerous to carry on having a home birth. I told them I would plan for a home birth up until the last few weeks then re-access my levels. Each time we were told that the senior consulting doctor would not allow a home birth, or that she would try to talk me out of it. I was meant to see this particular doctor three times and each time she was not available. Instead, I saw a lovely doctor who was shocked at my levels being so low, especially when I explained that I was still eating my usual diet. He said that although my levels were normal, and research didn't show that he should treat me any differently, common sense did! He wrote a lovely paragraph in my notes about me saying I was very reasonable and sensible about the whole affair. He said he was happy for a home birth if all continued to go so well, but I would still have to pass it through the senior consultant.

When you have Diabetes in pregnancy they won't let you go past your due date and will induce labour - if this happened it meant that I would not get my home birth. The kindly doctor booked me in to see the senior consultant the following week, four days past my due date. When I looked at my notes I saw that he had calculated that I was a week behind. We prayed before our appointment and were expecting a real battle with the senior consultant. My husband had the verse, 'in quietness and trust shall be our strength' (Isaiah 30:15). We had a scan first and again the baby was average size, the fluid was the correct amount and the placenta was getting enough blood. (An answer to more prayer, at the previous scan the fluid level had been creeping up). During the scan my husband got a word of knowledge and asked if the sonographer had any back trouble, she said she didn't. We went to the next room and my blood pressure and urine were tested. It was sent to the lab as they thought I may have a urine infection. The lead consultant we were due to see waltzed in to talk with a midwife and looked every bit as severe as we had heard, shifting the atmosphere of the nurses in the room to a heavy one. We went back to the waiting room and prayed some more. We were called in. Luke and I both said afterwards that we felt as though we could have sat with our mouths shut the entire meeting and we would have had the same outcome. We did not need to fight our corner at all. "It's not policy and I am obliged to advise you not to have a home birth. Why would you want to have a hospital birth? Hospitals are full of sick people, I'd want a home birth too. We offer induction but if you don't want one then that's fine. We just need to call paediatrics and ask them how best to test the baby's levels when he's born. With hospital births he would be monitored every

As we change our attitudes into 'can do' then we are in a position to overflow onto others and be used by God

two hours for the first twenty-four" is what she said to us, completely at ease and friendly, not at all what we expected. I agreed that I was happy to come in for daily monitoring as she noticed I was now past my due date. I knew it was unnecessary and a waste of my time but that it would put the hospital staff at ease: I was willing to be reasonable by going. God had really gone before us and changed her opinion. The next midwife we saw was amazed and confirmed that, "she usually shouts at people!" On our way out of her office Luke turned and asked if the lead consultant suffered with back pain, knowing that someone had to have a bad back as he had had the word of knowledge earlier. He explained where he felt the pain, as she was staring open mouthed at him, and he said that God wanted the pain to stop and wanted to heal her. She looked very shocked and said that she had just had major surgery on her back exactly where Luke had indicated. We offered to pray for her. She agreed but was more shocked when we turned back to pray immediately. She wouldn't let us pray with her then but we know that she'd had an encounter with a different perspective on God.

The paediatrician was not as friendly and really didn't want me to have a home birth. He gave no other information on why, just that it was against policy. He was extremely critical and it was not a pleasant dialogue. The midwife present was clearly irritated with him and argued our case for us. Once again we really didn't have to fight. We were peaceful about our decision. He made a plan for the midwife to check the baby's levels at birth then I was to bring him in if anything was wrong at all.

After birth, not only was our son under his anticipated weight; he showed no signs of Gestation Diabetes symptoms. The attending midwife said she would not even bother to check his levels as clearly he was perfectly well.

Medical staff are amazing, they do a fantastic job and have a rich amount of knowledge to guide us through pregnancy. My advice to anyone going through periods of bad reports from the doctors or midwives is to give yourself a deadline, (as long as doing so would not harm anyone). For example, had my levels been sky high it would not have been reasonable to assume that my faith was working. It clearly would not have been. I would have been putting myself and my baby at risk. I could reasonably give myself a two week window, I could get before God and pray in normal levels. But if after the two weeks I was still not seeing results, wisdom would listen to the medical staff and do what was policy. The aim is not to prove your faith, I could have still had a labour surrounded in the presence if I had been in hospital. The same is true for being induced, especially with Gestation Diabetes, I was comfortable going a week overdue, my first baby had been five days late. I gave myself a deadline of a week. From a place of peace I spoke over my body to go into labour within the week. However, had I not have I would have gone into the hospital to be induced, I had already agreed the date with the lead consultant. This decision was reasonable, it was putting the health of my baby above my desire for a natural start to labour. For me it's like the story in the Bible where David contends for the life of his sick child. He fasts and prays until the child dies, then he gets up and goes about his life (2 Samuel 12:16-24). Contend to see the standard, go after it full throttle within the deadline you or the doctors set. Push in to see it accomplished until the point of no return and if, for whatever reason, what you are contending for does not pull off, get up and carry on.

I want to emphasis here that the doctors, nurses, midwives and consultants are not working against you, they are doing their jobs and, for the most part, want you to succeed. They are trained to help you and have experience and training to back them up, we need them and their knowledge to help us through. Their purpose is to help you through, to keep you healthy and to deliver to you a healthy baby. Honour them, even if you are right, they are just doing their jobs. The goal is to have you both healthy, even if at the end of the day your faith is rocked or even shattered, I would rather that you listen to advice than to put yourself or your baby in harm's way.

11

In faith or not in faith?
That is the question

"In faith." is a term that we as Christians fling about in certain circles and I'm convinced that most of the time, no one knows one hundred percent what it means! We all nod back pretending that we indeed do know what it means, to be in faith!

Let's unpack this phrase 'in faith' then: it is being in a state of rest for the things you are believing for, unflappable in your assurance for what you are standing on. It is believing that there is no other possible outcome than the one you are in faith for, it is being sure and certain. Blindly declaring the Word is not faith, you first need to enter into Him, sit and let Him wash over you with His presence, receive the love and joy and peace that you find there. As you rest in Him you can see once again the clear promises that He has given you and that are laid out in His Word. If faith is the substance of things hoped for you can then stand on the promises and the love, joy and peace that you have received, faith is the evidence of the things you have received.

Faith is known by the person who is in it. However as I talk with different woman leading up to their births I often get a gut feeling, a sense, that it will not work out for them. It's difficult, when they say, "I'm in faith for this" to say, "I don't think you are!" In the main everything they are saying sounds like faith. They have scriptures and lists but I get a niggle, a discernment that they are not in faith. After delivery I ask them how it went and often they are disillusioned, hurt and blaming God. Their husbands are either joining them in their disappointed feelings, or are indifferent to the turmoil their wife is going through. Their labour was not as they were hoping. It is when talking to these woman, prior to delivery, that you can pick up on the language they are using. It is out of the overflow of the heart that the mouth speaks, (Matthew 12:34). When they are speaking you can glimpse what their heart is truly believing. Our words give direction to where we are heading, they set the course. You can pick up on where that trajectory is taking you by listening to the words you speak. It is never too late to set a new course, it can be done instantly, a quick repent and believe, turning one hundred and eighty degrees from the current course and choosing to believe and walk in what He has made available to us. It is closeness of relationship to the Godhead that keeps us on the right course. If we are continually in His presence we can then hear Him say, "this is the way, walk in it" (Isaiah 30:21), and readjust if we are slightly off. We are all on a continual journey of faith, making frequent adjustments to our views the more of His way we see revealed in front of us. We realign ourselves, our spirit man, and our soul to the author of life, to the One who knows how life should be lived to the full. As we learn to continually go back into His courts, into His presence, and remind ourselves of the perfect way, we recalibrate our balance as we connect to the source of life. Faith is knowing the faithful One, the One full of faith. It is not for us to become overly concerned whether we are 'in faith' or not for sickness and pain-free realities but it is being in Him which is what should consume us. Being in Him is the thing that assures us of our victory, because when we know Him we really know He has already won everything for us. 2 Corinthians 13:5-7 says, "Examine yourself to see whether you are in the faith; test yourself. Do you not realise that Christ Jesus is in you—unless, of

Spend a few moments and ask God if there are any areas in your thinking that need to change.

course, you fail the test? And I trust that you will discover that we have not failed the test. Now we pray to God that you will not do anything wrong—not so that people will see that we have stood the test but so that you will do what is right even though we may seem to have failed." We must be able to examine ourselves, the test is just to see if Jesus is in you, not whether you have passed or failed your faith venture. If you are saved Jesus is in you. Even though it may seem like you have failed, the test is to fall back into Jesus. From being in relationship with Him stems a persevering faith.

So how do we know whether we are in faith or not? As a third party I think it is easy to see if someone is in faith or not. What I have noticed through talking to women is that it's not necessarily what they say, but how they speak, and their paradigm of God's character. My experience has been that the more a woman KNOWS that God is good the more she sees happen in her labour. Faith takes the goodness of the heavenly realm to earth so you can be confident no matter what the circumstances, that you will see the goodness of the Lord in the land of the living (Psalm 27:13). The New King James version of the Bible says, "I would have lost heart, unless I had believed that I would see the goodness of the Lord in the land of the living". I believe if you have even a slight paradigm that says in bad circumstances, "this may be God's will or sovereign plan for me" then you have already lost ground, you can hear this viewpoint seeping through what woman say, even though it may not be directly said. Knowing that God is good gives the believer an assurance that you and God are pulling as a team, you are rooting for the same end. Without knowing He is good you *lose heart*, or as other translations of Psalm 27:13 say, *despair, faint* or *not believe*. Knowing His character has a direct impact on how we think He responds to us and what we are in faith for. It is imperative to know that what you are believing for matches up with what you think God is like.

It is not only what we say, but what we don't say that is a signpost to the level of our faith. A prime example would be the standard practice of not telling people you are pregnant until after at least twelve weeks gestation. I don't have anything against this but I don't particularly understand it. If you are pregnant; then you are! In our culturally crafted minds, we think of twelve weeks as being the beginning of the 'safe zone'. If you tell people you are pregnant, even at eight weeks, you will often hear, "Oh well it's early days yet." What is your reason for not telling people you are pregnant until a certain week? Is it based in fear? Are you waiting, holding your breath until you get to the safe zone? We have explored how negative words have an effect on our situations, if you flip the thinking then the more you confess that you are pregnant, the more positive you are, the more real it will become to you and your words of life will do just that. Speak life over your baby. You get on the offensive side of faith, your speaking life literally speaks living over your child, your confession of "I'm pregnant," reaffirms the truth even, I think, making miscarriage less likely.

We must take the Word of God and apply it directly to our circumstances, however diabolical they may seem, to ignore a bad situation or symptom will not change them. If you find yourself in a situation where you start to deny the facts, you are not in faith. You may be speaking life, but ignoring symptoms is just refusing to deal with them. However, as we use and apply the Word and our authority as sons of God, then we can actively have faith to see our circumstances come in line with His Word. If you are unwilling to address your negative circumstances then you are not in faith. Ephesians 1:21 says that Jesus is, "Far above all principality, and power, and might, and dominion, and every name that is named, not only in this world, but also in that which is to come." Naming something is important if Jesus and His Word (Psalm 138:2) are above everything that can be named. Identify the problem, speak it aloud and then directly speak the Word of God over it and see that superior reality become manifest instead of your bad circumstance.

As we use and apply the Word, and our authority as sons of God, then we can actively have faith to see our circumstances come in line with His Word

In Romans 4:18-25 it says, "Against all hope, Abraham in hope believed and so became the father of many nations, just as it had been said to him, *"So shall your offspring be."* Without weakening in his faith, he faced the fact that his body was as good as dead—since he was about a hundred years old—and that Sarah's womb was also dead. Yet he did not waver through unbelief regarding the promise of God, but was strengthened in his faith and gave glory to God, being fully persuaded that God had power to do what He had promised. This is why *"it was credited to him as righteousness."* The words *"it was credited to him"* were written not for him alone, but also for us, to whom God will credit righteousness, *"—for us who believe in Him who raised Jesus our Lord from the dead. He was delivered over to death for our sins and was raised to life for our justification."*

Abraham faced facts, but doing so did not rock his faith, it bolstered it. He knew that it would have to be supernatural; it would have to be God who accomplished this promise of a baby. He stood on the promises of God because he knew God to be powerful. God is the author of faith. Our authority works when we are looking at Him, not our situations. We must lift our eyes away from our circumstances onto Him who will give us the truth to apply directly onto our circumstances, changing their outcome. Abraham was credited for this act of faith and it says here that we will be also. I like the translation of verse twenty-three and twenty-four in the Message version of the Bible, "Abraham was declared fit before God by trusting God to set him right. But it's not just Abraham; it's also us! The same thing gets said about us when we embrace and believe the One who brought Jesus to life when the conditions were equally hopeless." Despite our circumstances, out of a place of knowing God and resting in His power, we are declared as fit before God. It all stems from this place of rest before Him who is able. In James 2:23 it says that Abraham was called God's friend because of His faith: we too are friends of God. Abraham was human and initially he did doubt. He and Sarah took the promise and tried to make it happen themselves.

How good are you at looking at the facts without getting overwhelmed by them?

When you have times of doubt you can still win. If our faith is shaken, or we doubt, the promise still holds if we choose to come back in line with it. Regardless of our failure we are still a friend of God and honoured for our faith, because when we turn from trying to do something ourselves which is acting from unbelief which is sin, we repent and our sin is forgiven and we are restored back to our place of honour.

Faith can be easy in short bursts. When I read for the first time about the possibility of a heavenly standard in childbirth my faith spiked, living it out on a daily basis was a little more challenging, which is why I wrote a journal to accompany this book. Unless you actively seek to maintain faith it fizzles out. Unless we fill ourselves and keep filling ourselves with truth, then other things will fill that space instead. Pregnancy is like a nine month training period for the biggest faith race of your life! We need to exercise faith, push its boundaries in our life, just the way you would push your body if you were preparing for a literal race. You cannot expect, at month four of pregnancy to get the "I can have a supernatural childbirth" revelation, letting it sit with you, thinking of it occasionally, even having a couple of prayer 'post its' around for the next four months, then as your due date roles around start to cram faith talk, lists and prayers, expect to pull off a supernatural childbirth. Why not? It wouldn't work for a real race so let's be wise in the spirit also. Let's prepare. The preparation is not so much speaking life, believing, confessing and meditating on Him, although that is a part of it. I don't want you to come away from this book thinking that if you put all the principles into action that you will automatically have the desired result. If you are simply following the ritual or formula, then it doesn't come from personal revelation, it is knowing truth that sets you free. When something of Heaven is revealed to you, grace is also released to enable the Word to be fulfilled. The preparation I am referring to is more about a process of us renewing our minds than striving to obtain the standard. Strife will get us nowhere because strife is not faith. Faith is birthed in rest. Everything must come from the rest of knowing what is available to us, as ones who are seated in heavenly places, through what Christ has done for us. We rest in His finished work of the cross. But faith comes from a revelation, truth revealed to us so that it is really known to us, that is how we can be sure and certain and therefore 'in faith'.

I just want to add here, if you are reading this book for the first time and you are almost at your due date. It is never too late to receive grace. He is faithful and you are therefore able to have a supernatural standard in pregnancy and labour even if you were not aware prior to this point. Whether you have prepared or not His grace is sufficient for you. It is as truth is revealed to you that faith comes. It's like a light bulb turning on inside; it becomes clear that this is available and obtainable. It is from the place of His presence that we rest and receive the grace to accomplish what is available. You absolutely can have a supernatural childbirth without preparation because He is able to fulfil His Word in your life as you understand that that is what you can have. Grace is not dependent on timing, you can get a divine download and faith can be immediate. Being willing to go after what has been revealed to you is more important than fulfilling the principles. It becomes about His grace and enablement. It's like the workers in the field who all pitched up at different times but got paid the same amount because of the grace of the owner (Matthew 20:1-16). No matter when you start believing you can have the same outcome and experience as someone who has been preparing and renewing their mind for nine months or longer. But should we abuse grace and not bother to prepare? No! (Romans 6:15).

This process of mind renewal is how we manage the revelation we have been entrusted with. If our experience had been different, if Eve had had a pain-free birth, followed by every other woman in history doing the same until now, we wouldn't need to prepare to have a pain-free birth. Pain-free birth would be normal and therefore expected. You wouldn't even consider that it could be painful, just like we don't expect to feel pain when we drink a glass of water; it wouldn't cross our minds to prepare to drink it! So if your mind is renewed, as Christ has enabled us to have His mind, (1 Corinthians 2:16), then we can have a supernatural birth without 'post it' scriptures and daily confession. But even if at the point you understood that this standard in pregnancy and labour was possible, you shut yourself away from all people and propaganda about painful labour and alike, for the remainder of your gestation you would still be living with all of history's previous experience and misguided information. Therefore, we must renew our minds, living in the world but not of it. As a mind thinks so is the person (Proverbs 23:7 NKJ). We must renew our thoughts so that we can have a different outcome than the world's standard. It should become easier, as we understand that what He has won for us should be normal to us. As we begin to live in that reality, the next time we believe for the same thing we don't need to prepare in the same way. If you have had one supernatural childbirth then it will be easier to go on to have another one next time round, because there will be a certain amount of the revelation that is real truth to you. However "be careful you don't fall" (1 Corinthians 10:12). We have to take care of the precious seed of revelation. We have to gate-keep our minds: it's a battle at times but we win it through rest in what He has already done. Bill Johnson, (from Bethel church in Redding, California) often says that "you know when your mind is renewed when the impossible looks logical." To a certain degree you can tell if you are in faith for a pain-free labour, because it feels like the only and obvious outcome.

So what is the key to faith? Empowerment. A grace that enables you to do something you couldn't do before. My two favourite principles are presence and tenacity. Empowerment comes from God, from His presence. It is here that we find all we need for life and Godliness (2 Peter 1:3). You can only maintain faith, hope and tenacity for a few days or weeks. In the rest of His presence we find the enablement for faith, grace. His grace is sufficient for us (2 Corinthians 12:9). His grace is His powerful ability and God is both powerful and able! We do not need to be striving to work up faith. Grace works when we are weak and makes us strong. So how do you get this enablement, this grace? By receiving it. Grace is found in His presence, before His throne of grace. Boldly come to His throne of grace and receive all that He has won for you. Salvation is a free gift, grace is part of this salvation gift; it's what enables us to 'do' the saved life! Hebrews 4:15-16, "For we do not have a high priest who is unable to empathise with our weaknesses, but we have one who has been tempted in every way, just as we are—yet He did not sin. Let us then approach God's throne of grace with confidence, so that we may receive mercy and find grace to help us in our time of need." It comes back to falling into His unending presence as we come before Him, just being our own weak self, resting in His able power and being graced with that power to do great exploits. Faith works from this place in His presence, *God is love*, the atmosphere in His presence is love. As we look upon Him, as we fall more in love with Him, as we become aware of love, as we are draped in love, as we cultivate this love relationship, faith works. These verses in Galatians 5:4-6, tell us that faith works only through love, not from law, formula or ritual but from relationship. "You who are trying to be justified by the law have been alienated from Christ; you have fallen away from grace. For through the Spirit we eagerly await by faith the righteousness for which we hope... The only thing that counts is faith expressing itself through love." If we start to strive for the principles to work in our lives, we alienate ourselves from the very source of faith that makes the principles become reality. The only thing that counts, the only thing that works, is faith working through a mutual love relationship between you and God. So concentrate not on claiming and confessing, although that is part of it, but instead on the One who loves you, the One who is working for your good and expected end (Jeremiah 29:11). Faith is the substance of things hoped for (Hebrews 11:1). Let us put our hope, not on the principles: let us put our hope in God because we know Him to be good.

If we start to strive for the principles to work in our lives, we alienate ourselves from the very source of faith that make the principles become reality. The only thing that counts, the only thing that works, is faith working through a mutual love relationship with you and God.

As we know God and let Him reveal Himself to us. As we fall in love with Him, faith gets so rooted in us that we become sure and certain. Certain of who He is. Certain of His character, certain of what He has won, certain of who we are, certain of the grace He has given us, certain then of the power we have, certain of our outcome because of our certainty in Him. It's a deep assurance, a substance that gives us strength at our core. It's in His presence that we get to know Him. Those who know God do great exploits (Daniel 11:32 KJV). Do you know God? Are you dwelling in His presence? Are you tenacious for what you know of Him? Are you tenacious for what that knowing enables you to receive? Are you in deep rooted faith?

If you find out now that you are not in faith, don't worry because you have time to become so, however short a time you have left. It takes no time at all to let a tenacious faith from Holy Spirit take root in your being. God is gracious by nature. Repent if you have been lying to yourself and see God take you from strength to strength. In your weakness He proves Himself strong. If you are not honest with yourself then you may end up realising that you were not in faith, but it will be after the event and then you have to deal with disappointment. However, even in disappointment your faith can be restored, we have a redemptive God. He never wants us to go through bad experiences - no father wants that for their children. In time, when reflecting back on a bad experience, we will see the hand of God throughout our tough ordeal. He will teach us from our bad experience and tough circumstances, but I believe with all my heart, it is not in His nature to make us go through them in order to teach us something. He makes the very best of every situation we walk through. Even if we miss the mark He turns everything around for our good (Romans 8:28). He teaches us and challenges us so that next time we will finish the race. Hebrew 12:1-2, "therefore, since we are surrounded by such a great cloud of witnesses, let us throw off everything that hinders and the sin that so easily entangles. And let us run with perseverance the race marked out for us, fixing our eyes on Jesus, the pioneer and perfecter of faith. For the joy set before Him He endured the cross, scorning its shame, and sat down at the right hand of the throne of

God." Faith can sometimes feel like an endurance test! It is a journey that can feel like a marathon at times, but we have the choice to continue to believe even in the midst of wanting to quit. In labour particularly, persevere, don't give up at the first hurdle you didn't expect to get in your way. If you have one painful contraction then seek His presence, pick yourself back up and persevere to see the next contraction be pain-free. Never give in, pray on every occasion (Ephesians 6:18), even in the midst of a tough labour or circumstance, be alert for possible hurdles but never give up when you feel resistance.

Faith and even persevering come from rest, *"let us not strive to work up faith but simply stir the gift that is already within us"* (2 Timothy 1:6). We only need a minuscule amount of faith to see mighty things accomplished (Matthew 17:20). Faith is a gift that we have already been given (Ephesians 2:8), we don't need to exert ourselves, or go blue in the face asking for what we already have. Believe that you have received it (Mark 11:24). We have all been given a measure of faith: guard and manage your heart. Feel the gift of faith stir within you until it whips into an unstoppable whirlwind. You stir the gift by getting revelation from His Word, because faith comes by hearing (Romans 10:17). Faith is the basis of The Faith, it's not unobtainable.

> *Faith and even persevering come from rest, let us not strive to work up faith but simply stir the gift that is already within us*

Get into a place of His presence, of peace and ask yourself the following questions. Answer honestly because it is only you who will lose out if you do not. I want for you to KNOW that you are in faith, I want you to avoid the disappointment after birth of realising that you weren't. I am not trying to rock your faith but test your walls. It is better to realise now if you need to firm up the walls of your shield of faith, than to deal with the rubble of a crumbled fortress after a bad experience.

Ask yourself the following questions:

What is the language I use when talking about pregnancy and labour?

Is it sure and certain?

Is it void of confidence?

Does what I say match what my heart is feeling?

Does what I say come from my revelation?

If I am told what I am believing is not possible, what rises up on the inside of me?

Do I go after what I am believing for?

Am I actively believing each day?

Am I consistent in what I say?

Do I believe that God will ever place me in harm's way?

Do I believe that God wants me to experience pain or trauma?

Am I willing to look at my negative circumstances?

Do I believe He has done it and won it for me?

Is sickness and pain my inheritance?

12

Great expectations:
Trust God not Google

Information, I think, is a large key to success in faith. If you know what your body has to do then you are off to a great start. During my first labour after two hours of contractions my body started to push, it shocked me. Nothing I had read had prepared me for this different sensation between phases of labour. Fear set in and the contraction hurt before I remembered what I had read, my body was entering the next stage of labour. I gained control of my thoughts and the next contraction was intense but with no pain. If I had had no prior information of what my body had to do, the different sensation would have freaked me out so much that fear would have made the remainder of my experience a very different one. Go to the library, look on the internet, and read all you can about what to expect. Attend antenatal classes, talk to your midwife and swot up. I have been told that midwives generally have better experiences giving birth than the rest of us, I think it is because they are armed with information about what they have to do. We don't have to trust the information, our trust is in God not Google, but we can be armed with information to help us along our journeys.

However with all this information comes much negativity. Your ante-natal classes will be filled with bad stories and implement demonstrations! In mine we had a whole week on 'what can go wrong'. Have an opinion on whether you want certain pain killers, even if you are expecting not to need any. I was in faith to have a pain-free labour with my first baby but I wanted to have a back up plan in case either my circumstances changed, or my faith did not work! Because I was having a home birth and no pain killers would be available if I needed them I hired a TENs machine from the hospital, (it's a hand held machine that you hook up to send pulses through your body that are said to help with pain) and the midwife brought gas and air with her. I didn't need either but they were there if I did end up needing them. During labour is not the time you want to be discussing with the midwife what you do and don't want! Have your requirements in your birthing plan to make the process less complicated if you do end up needing pain relief. My birthing plan was something like, "I want to labour with no pain relief but if needed I will ask for gas and air." This didn't undermine my faith that I would have a pain-free labour. Especially when having your first baby, when things are so unknown, it's just wisdom to understand the process and glance at the information about pain killers and procedures. When you've already been through a birth you might not want to put anything in your plan, I don't think I did for my second labour. Some woman do have pain, that's not the standard that you may be aiming at but if for whatever reason that standard is not reached then knowing the process is a benefit. It's a difficult balance and sometimes people think you are not in faith if you contemplate the possibility that it won't go according to plan. I am a very realistic person and I don't find it difficult to plan for both, but it is a very fine line where you need to be very self-aware to address if you are in faith or fear. It's like the woman in Luke eight with the issue of blood. Jesus knew that out of the thousand that had touched Him, one had done so in faith. The others around Jesus would have certainly been touching Him, some perhaps hoping to receive something, but only one got the healing because she reached out in faith. She was in faith: had no back up plan: Jesus had to come through for her. If in your mind you keep having "what if" thoughts about what could go wrong then chances are that you are working from a place of fear. We need to trust Him. Information can also spiral you into a place of fear for what could go wrong. I looked at it from a studying perspective. Stepping back a little from 'this is about my labour' and just digested the medical information. I had at one point wanted to study as a midwife and found everything fascinating. If you can distance yourself, the information you gain is a big key to success.

Labour is about delivering a healthy baby to a healthy mother. Nothing more. If you can maintain a heavenly standard, then your experience will be a more pleasurable one, and you will be able to share God's goodness through your testimony, but nothing more. You will not have failed if you experience pain. Jesus walked on water, the Bible tells us that we can do the same and even greater things than Christ if we choose to go after them (John 14:12). Walking on water is outside our normal experience but then so too is a pain-free labour for most. This unnatural, or supernatural reality is open to us too but when someone tries to walk on water and falls in the lake we don't see it as a failure. We laugh! In the same way we need to lighten up about labour and give it a go! Be honest with yourself, if during labour you begin to lose the reality of Heaven, if it hurts, take pain relief. No one is marking you, you are not out to win a prize. If you are in pain then say so and do what you need to do to have a healthy child and be a healthy mother. Healthy is more than just in your body but your mind also. If you experience pain you can still have a supernatural labour, supernatural is not just pain-free. It is getting revelation from God about your labour and its circumstances and seeing it manifest. Pain- free is definitely available and is the obtainable standard set by the cross, but there are many other things that make up a supernatural experience in labour. Go after it all but if you don't get some aspects that's okay, the ones you did get are still supernatural. Supernatural is God being involved in the natural.

What do you dream of doing that is "greater than Jesus did"?

During my first labour I had a few painful contractions. I didn't ask for pain relief as the midwife wasn't there, actually I didn't even think about wanting any. I was confident that if I could re-align myself with Heaven's standard then the next contraction would be pain-free again. I calmed down into peace by focusing on Jesus' face. I became aware of His presence and drew from the peace that is found in His atmosphere. A determination to persevere bubbled inside and I was then able to regain the pain- free reality of Heaven. If, however, my pain had lasted for more than a few contractions I would have got pain relief when I could. Instead I got a little obstinate and slapped the wall! I spoke to my body, I rebuked the pain and the devil for meddling, and I spoke life into the situation, claiming the next contraction to be painless. I think these two things are the path to seeing what you believe. Peace from His presence and tenacity from knowing what He has won. I think that these, twinned with a healthy dose of realism makes you a level headed person of faith!

Practically, during contractions, if you feel your focus shifting, take a deep breath: I found this helpful. Focus, in your mind's eye on Jesus, or something you can imagine, using scripture, like the throne of Father God. As what I saw in my mind became more real, my peace returned. At other times I would quote scriptures quietly to myself as they came to mind, or I would wander over to the bathroom mirror full of scripture post-its and looking myself in the eye, I would confess them. Hearing the Word increased my faith and reminded me what I was standing for and perseverance kicked in. In my second labour I used worship music to connect into heavenly places. Depending on the song, the lyrics would either paint a picture of Heaven that I could meditate on, or through worship of the Lord I would be caught up into His courts and then receive the grace and mercy that was all around His throne. Whatever works for you to see, hear, feel or be conscious of, the reality of Heaven is great, there is no right or wrong. It's all about a relationship with Him.

As what I saw in my mind became more real then my peace returned

If you think this sounds a little like Hypno-birth then you would be right! Would I train in Hypno-birth or advise anyone else to do so?

No! Your midwife may have some understanding of what you are doing if you say you are wanting to use your own version of 'Hypo-birth' during labour. They will have a grid for that terminology, so use it if you wish. Much of the 'new age' movement is counterfeit from God's original plan; close but not the real thing. The devil is not creative by nature, he can only distort what God has already created. Focusing your mind is not a modern or new age concept, we are to set our minds on things above, (Colossians 3:1-4), meditation on God is biblically grounded, (for example, Psalm 1:2, Joshua 1:8, Psalm 48:9, Psalm 119:27). The issue with Hypno-birth is that you focus on the wrong thing and can therefore open up the spiritual realm through the wrong access. This illegal access gives the enemy a door into your life that is far better left shut! Let's make Jesus our focus and then we know we are safe; but let's not be

> *The way is opened up but engaging with Him and that's up to you*

afraid to use things that can seem to follow current fad or weird practice. Search the Bible and do what it says there, even if the devil has copied its technique and used it to lead people astray from God's original intention. God has given us Holy Spirit to lead us into heavenly places, He is our guide and Jesus is our doorway. If we keep focused on Him then no other spirit can deserve us or take us through an illegal entrance. Let's take back what was originally ours.

What are we expecting labour to look like? How will you know when you are in labour? If you feel no pain then what are you expecting to feel so that you know when to call the hospital? These are questions asked by all first time mums regardless of whether or not they are believing for no pain. All the reading in the world can't totally prepare you for how labour will feel for you. I think each woman experiences something slightly different but some things remain the same. Contractions, when not twinned with pain, feel like tightenings across your belly, back and sometimes thighs. It's a little like a period cramp but pain-free. It's sort of uncomfortable and your whole body does it without you doing anything. I have heard that for some people the tightness ripples over them and others it is more of a sudden clench. Everybody's threshold for pain is different. Some people think that if you do not have pain in labour it's because they can endure a higher level of pain. I do understand that everyone experiences pain on different levels, and I know that some people find it easy to block out pain in the way that they think about it during the moment. For some people however this is not the case. When pain comes and you cannot contain it or you lose control, you will come under it. If you can, when experiencing pain, remain logical in your thoughts as best you can, isolate the pain enough that you can say no to it. You will find peace again in Jesus. Having said that, pain is still pain if you can suppress it or not. I don't think that Jesus taking our pain means that we are just to suppress it. It means He took it; it is no longer there for us to feel. So as we come into our heavenly pain-free reality we can have just that, a pain-free reality on earth.

A good example of the sensation of labour is when you contract another muscle in your body, such as doing a sit-up. You can crunch up and hold your position, your muscles are tight and if you hold it for a long while you begin to shake, it's uncomfortable, it can become intense and you can even want to give in, but it's not painful. The term 'supernatural childbirth' can conjure up a very quick easy event, with a light from Heaven beaming down upon you! Labour, I found, was not 'easy' or a walk in the park. It was hard work, strenuous, and a little uncomfortable. God was completely there but not in a beam of light! Engaging with Him was up to me, just like in everyday life. The initial tightenings that can come and go slowly, eventually build until they are intense. Not painful, intense. They build in pressure and repetitiveness and last longer. At the beginning you may be walking around and "Ooh. I think that was one." By the end however the intensity takes your breath away and all your focus goes onto the contraction. You cannot walk and you know you are having one! Keep breathing and have your mind focused on Heaven. For example, if you pray in tongues you don't know what you are saying, but you can engage your mind and have understanding at the same time you are speaking in a foreign tongue. Engaging your mind helps you stay focused and makes you aware of what God is doing and

Holy Spirit is praying through you. The same is true for labour. As you have a contraction engage your mind and let your thoughts dwell on things above. You can even pray in tongues, go to English then return to tongues again. If at the end it is too intense to concentrate, declare, "Thank you Jesus" repeatedly in your head, or something similar; this will help focus you. You can also practice turning your attention to what is happening in the spiritual realm of the room. Where is Jesus in the room? Focus on His face. What are the angels doing? Angels are ministers of God sent for our benefit (Genesis 19:15-16, Hebrews 1:14, Matthew 4:11, Psalm 91:11-12). They are also at our disposal, (1 Peter 3:22, tells us that angels are in submission to Jesus, and we now have the same authority as Jesus as co-heirs with Him). Their purpose is to carry out the words of the Father (Psalm 103:20). We as Sons of God speak out His decrees, so therefore at His Word in our mouths the angels are commissioned. We do not place our focus on the angelic, they are not to be worshiped, but equally they are not to be ignored. You have the authority to send the angels to do what you need them to, and as you pray they fulfil your prayer. So if in labour you need the midwife to arrive sooner, or your husband needs to come home quickly from work to be with you, speak out "traffic move freely and allow them through, lights turn green at the right moment". It is the angels that respond and move the traffic at your word.

As you become aware of the realm of Heaven invading earth through the words you speak, everything becomes possible. If you feel a negative atmosphere when you arrive at the hospital speak out the opposite, "I speak joy and hope into the atmosphere". Ministering angels start to minister that joy and hope to the staff and women around you. You can

You can affect the labour of the other woman on the maternity ward just by being in proximity to them.

actually affect the labour of the other women in the maternity ward just by being in proximity to them. (Just like Peter's shadow affected those he walked past, Acts 5:15-16).

Oral Roberts tells his story in his book *"When you see the invisible, you can do the impossible."*[2] Just before the birth of his third child,

Oral was doing a crusade. At the end of the crusade he was meant to drive straight home for the due date of his baby three days later on the Wednesday. As the crusade was drawing to a close it was clear that God had not finished His work there and the local pastors asked Roberts, "If you could just give us three more days, we believe more than a thousand souls will be saved, besides large numbers receiving their healing from the hand of the Lord. Can't you and your wife postpone your baby's birth in order for this to happen?" What a ludicrous suggestion! Roberts answered exclaiming "postpone the baby's birth! ...How could we postpone it?" All manner of thoughts ran through his head as he pondered about what the pastors had said and how his wife would respond. But as they stood and prayed peace came with the presence of God and Oral began to understand that if God was supernaturally healing people at the crusade then He could delay his baby's birth. He called his wife and broke the news, asking if she would partner with him and agree together that the birth would be delayed. She amazingly agreed and they set a deadline for the baby to be born before midnight on the Friday and asked God to do the impossible. The crusade was a great success as they had thought. Oral drove home and on the Friday they went to the hospital, knowing that it was now time. When they arrived the nurse would not call the doctor as the baby was not on his way. Mrs Roberts assured her it was and asked her again to call the doctor, the nurse refused but they stayed in the hospital. The Roberts walked the hallway and prayed holding to the agreement they had made of a pre-midnight deadline. Within minutes contractions were very strong and Oral's wife was whisked away to the delivery room.

Often it is at the final stage of pregnancy that we can lose our focus. Both my babies were late. In those days post due date you can start to: slip into striving, willing the baby to come: become disillusioned that you are not going into labour. We must run the race to the end and never give up hope at the last hurdle. Continue to stand on the things that you have agreed with God about your birth, continue to rest in His goodness. The title of Oral's book , "When you see the invisible, you can do the impossible" is the key. We draw our strength from knowing Him, as we spend time in His presence we see the invisible realm of Heaven, we can then do the impossible because the impossible looks normal in the realm that we are seated in. Continue to fall back into Him, especially if you find yourself going past your due date. Stand on His promises and stay in His rest, knowing that He who has begun the work in you will see it through to completion (Philippians 1:6). He will never abandon you, so draw closer to Him. If you prepare yourself in the natural through information, practice being in the presence and cultivate a close relationship with God leading up to your labour, connect with Him during it. The truth is there is nothing to fear, He is capable of doing far more than you can ask or imagine (Ephesians 3:20). All things are possible with God (Matthew 19:26).

If through this book you take one thing away with you for your labour, I would hope that it would be the value of living in the presence. If you can maintain the presence of God in your labour then as far as I'm concerned you've won. Even if you are experiencing pain, and other circumstances are not matching up to what you had hoped, if you are able to dial down the noise of your surroundings and focus on Him and His presence around you, then Heaven invades the earth and Heaven's reality will be more real to you. Like when Stephen was being stoned, as he was more aware of Heaven than what was being done to his body. If you have a painful contraction and immediately get yourself refocused on Him you can expect the next contraction to be pain-free, rather than giving up. If you give into pain, you resign yourself that you've lost your goal, the fight goes out of you as you focus on what your body is feeling, rather than maintaining your grasp on Heaven's pain-free reality. If you immerse yourself in the place of His presence throughout your labour, if you are able to roll with the punches of what is happening around you and not be rocked by your circumstances then I think you will have the best labour. It's a little like a dancer who prepares for a show: during the performance she may trip or stumble from the original dance she had prepared but because it's for an audience she doesn't falter, she listens to the rhythm of the music and manages to incorporate her mistake into the beauty of the dance. Through labour we can do the same, we can have something happen that we weren't expecting or hadn't planned for, but if we can keep our ears attuned to the rhythm of Heaven then we can flow from one step to the other flawlessly.

✦

13

From me to you:

S.W.A.L.K

Beth-Annily is my eldest child. Shortly after her birth I wrote her a letter to read at a time when she could understand. This is the account of her birth.

Dear Beth-Annily,

I woke up the day you were born knowing that it was a different day. It was a Sunday and Daddy and I were leading worship at Church that morning. My tummy started to tighten and I knew that I would meet you soon. No one could wipe the smile from my face! We arranged cover for the band and went downstairs to make banana smoothies and inflate the birthing pool that would receive you into the world, at our home in London, England.

Daddy called the midwife and she came at eleven to see how you and I were doing. I lay on the couch and she felt my tummy to see which way you were laying. You had put yourself in the perfect position and I was thankful because this was something I had told you to do, it was your first act of obedience! I had a very strong contraction but the midwife thought that you would not come today because I was not in enough pain and the contractions had to become more intense.

But you and I knew better didn't we Bubba. We could feel that today was a special day, one of new beginnings, it was the eighth after all, the number representing new things. I was believing God's Word and I knew that I wasn't expecting pain but I understood that more 'intense' and 'pain' didn't have to be the same thing.

My body did what it was supposed to do, just the way I had told it to in all the days leading up to this birth day. At Midday the more intense contractions had come and my body was doing a great job of regulating my breathing. It also decided that it did not need to process the banana smoothie and give birth at the same time so it got rid of it! Daddy called the midwife again and she wanted to speak to me. She was surprised that today was indeed the day and commented on how quickly things had progressed. She congratulated me for my good breathing and said that she would be with us in a couple of hours after a few house calls. I said okay but smiled knowing it would not be that long.

I was in no pain but the contractions were consuming and hard work. I thought that the TENS machine I had hired might help with the intensity so Daddy helped put the pads on my back and turned up the dial. Pain shot though my back and rippled to my tummy. I shouted at Daddy, (poor Daddy) he took the pads off immediately. You see, my trust had gone from our Jesus to a machine and the pain had come.

At twelve twenty I tried to push you out twice. The first time I got scared and it hurt. Again my focus had gone from Jesus and onto fear. Fear is an enemy of faith. I slapped the wall and determination set in as I rebuked the pain. I got back into peace quickly after only having two painful contractions. Daddy called the midwife again. She didn't want to speak to me this time as she could hear what was happening in the background. I had thought that the process of labour for me would be quiet, but I was very wrong!* Sometimes things don't go the way you expect! I was just glad for the neighbours' sake that it was in the middle of the day and not in the middle of the night, especially since it was so hot that all the windows were open! Even in my focused state I was embarrassed, aware that the neighbours were having a summer BBQ!

I was internally praying that Jesus would take me to Heaven so that I would be so involved in His presence that nothing else would matter. I said this out loud once and you should have seen the look on Daddy's face, he thought the pain must be so bad that I wanted to die. I couldn't stop laughing!

The midwife, Jill, was stunned that you were on your way so quickly and rushed to us within fifteen minutes. I have never seen anyone put on an apron so fast, or lay down sheets so quickly!

My contractions were now on top of each other and I couldn't lay down for her to check me. I could hear our neighbour friends downstairs scurrying to fill the birthing pool, but I was chuckling internally because I knew that I would not be able to make it downstairs to use it, by now the contractions took my breath away and I had to stop walking, they were coming so close together that walking down our very narrow steep stairs would have been dangerous. The midwife asked Daddy to get the gas and air from her car, despite my telling her that I would not need it. She asked if it could be in the room just in case and I agreed because its presence wouldn't rock my faith. I knew we wouldn't need it, I wasn't in any pain.

The second midwife arrived and I smiled. I had seen her in the hospital the week before and had thought to myself that she would be lovely to have at your birth. I had not realised that God would hear my thought and answer that unspoken request. You see, God sees the desires of your heart however small they are. This was a little sign for me that God was and wanted to be involved in your birth.

At the end of the pushing I was so impatient to see you, I had waited nine months for this moment and the suspense was too much! I screamed "come on" at the top of my lungs then started to laugh heartily with each push. I remember thinking how ridiculous it was that I was having a laughing fit when I should be focused, but I just couldn't stop it. I was groaning pretty loudly at this point and Daddy bent down to look at my face and was so relieved to see me beaming. He was funny to watch because he was fascinated with the whole process and was also impatient to finally lay eyes on you! Daddy started to pray in tongues at one point and I quickly asked him to stop. He wasn't doing anything wrong but I became more aware of what the midwives would think rather than staying in the Lord's peaceful presence.

Your head started to crown and Jill asked if I wanted to touch your hair. At first I didn't as I was concentrating hard, but then I did and it gave me fresh energy. I was so excited I pushed again and you came out! I lay down and gave you a cuddle, I couldn't believe that you were mine.

The midwife told me some bad news. She said that because you had had your hand by your head I had torn and it was a three degree tear. I would have to go to hospital by ambulance and probably stay over night. I didn't want to leave Daddy on our first night together as a family, so when I was in the shower I prayed, I was not going to let the devil score points. I asked God to send help from His sanctuary and He did. When I was examined again the wound was not half as bad and I was able to be stitched at home.

While the midwife did the stitches, Jesus answered my prayer and took me to Heaven. I knew what was happening in the natural and could answer the occasional question from the midwife. Heaven became more real to me in that moment, it was like having a dream while being awake.

Jesus greeted me before a lake so crystal clear that I could see all the fish and mammals beneath the water. He reached out and took my hand and led me on top of the water. As we walked the water became solid but just in front of us the animals began to dance together and jump out of the water. I asked the Lord what this was and He said that they were excited about you being born. He said that all creation rejoiced at your arrival! I began to cry on my bed at home and Jill asked if I was okay. She did not realise why I was crying, I was overwhelmed with the joy in Heaven. Jesus led me onto the shore and across the water. Above us was a golden castle and below our feet was not sand but millions of pearls of different shapes and sizes. He said these were my pearls produced under great pressure.

Jill told me that I would need to take painkillers for the stitches and that I would take a while to heal, but I said to myself that I would have a testimony, that would give the glory to Jesus. I was never in pain and never needed any pain killers for the stitches. But why did I tear in the first place? Looking back I realise that it was the one thing I feared. I took the scriptures stuck around our house about quick birth and being a joyful mother of children, but I never really believed I would not tear. I would chant "do not rip, you will not tear..." over my body but I was in fear not faith. However, God was faithful even in my failure and did indeed get His testimony.

My prayer is that you and I can live in this kind of supernatural lifestyle in our daily lives. Giving birth to you was a joy! It was not what people spoke over me that happened, but what I believed. I know that seeing you grow will also be my joy in every stage of your life. You are truly a blessing to me my daughter. I love you.

Love Your Mummy   Xx

* (For me, as the contractions became more intense it felt like I was pushing a large truck up hill all by myself, as I pushed I found it easy to focus by letting out an 'arrrrhhh' shout as if someone would as they exert energy pushing a truck uphill).

✦

14

Unexpected:

Unassisted birth

My first child Beth-Annily was born at home. Eight hours of labour from first twinge to delivery, and only three hours of established labour. Every contraction, bar three were completely pain-free. Only when my focus slipped from God to fear, did the pain come and it was painful! Even though I didn't have time to get into the birthing pool as I'd wanted, the joy of creating and birthing someone into the world was so overwhelming that I was laughing throughout my last few pushes. I believe I experienced a supernatural childbirth.

Giving birth to my son, Reuben-River was a very different experience but just as powerful. My due date was the First of February and I'd had three nights of false labour randomly from the beginning of January. On the last of these tiring evenings I told my body enough was enough. I prayed that the next time I had a contraction I would go into labour for real, no more false starts. Another day passed. As I was overdue and in a high risk category for Gestation Diabetes I needed to attend daily monitoring at the hospital. There had been some confusion from the previous day about whether I had a urine infection but they now assured me that I didn't.

At one in the morning on the Seventh of February I woke up with a stabbing pain to the side of my stomach. Thinking I must have an infection after all I took a couple pain killers, went to the loo and went back to bed. I woke again at one thirty with the same pain. It took me two more of these pains at ten minutes apart to twig it was labour! It felt very different from my last birth, not just because I was feeling pain but the sensations of the contractions were in completely different areas. I progressed very quickly to five minutes apart; each time the same stabbing pain came. I was eventually able to leave the bathroom at two thirty to wake my husband. He put on some music and laid down sheets, and within the next two contractions they were coming every three minutes. I decided to wait before calling the hospital, as I had not had a bloody show, like with my first labour. I also wanted to regain my reality on Heaven so that the pain would stop and I wanted to do that without a stranger watching as I knew this would make me feel self-conscious. I should have called!

My labour felt entirely different this time around. I experienced my contractions in my thighs and although I didn't feel I was going to die, like some women describe, I was definitely experiencing pain. My focus however remained on Jesus, the one who died so I didn't have to have pain. With every fresh contraction I expected that no pain would come. Just before four in the morning I pushed and realised we still had not called for a midwife. Luke contacted the hospital and then phoned my Mom to fetch our sleeping daughter. I suddenly felt prompted to run a bath. I asked Luke to run one but he was getting our daughter's bag ready. I was going to wait but felt an urgency to run the bath. I got in, had a contraction as I heard my daughter say, "Bye bye Mummy" as my Mom carried her to the car. Luke then came back in and I had another contraction. I knew I was close to delivering. I reached down and felt my baby's head full of hair. "She's not going to be here in time, I can feel his head" was all I could get out between contractions. I knew what I had said hadn't registered with my husband as he continued to scoop gunk out of the water. Another contraction immediately followed, and suddenly our son shot out. It all happened in slow motion, as the realisation hit that what I saw wasn't more mucus but my baby!

I picked him up, and looked up seeing Luke mirroring my shocked expression. I laughed once "quick, towels!" The surreal slow motion stopped as Reuben-River took his first breath. Luke rang the midwife to inform her she was late! She arrived seven minutes later to clear up! He was born in three hours sixteen minutes from first contraction or two hours twenty-one minutes of established labour.

After having my first baby, Beth-Annily, quickly, and the midwife only being with us for the final pushing stage of labour, I commented on how funny it was, not expecting it would happen again. I had been meditating on Exodus one where it says the *"Hebrew women are strong and lively and are quick at giving birth before the midwives can get to them."* Back at the beginning of my second pregnancy I just had a feeling that this actually would be the case for us this time. By the end of the pregnancy I had forgotten about my 'feeling.' My feeling was God informing me what would happen! It should have prompted me to call the hospital sooner than we did.

God is always speaking but are we in the place to listen to His gentle nudging?

For my second labour the main things I was believing for were; a pain-free, quick home birth, under three hours, with a maximum of ten pushes (I pushed Beth-Annily out for over an hour, and my muscles were very sore the following few days). I was believing that: my baby would not be affected by the Gestation Diabetes I had been diagnosed with; all the after care needed would be done at home; I would not tear or have any grazes; baby would feed well and immediately and also that my milk would be plentiful as this had been an issue with my daughter.

Did I get everything that I was believing for? No. Does it change the way that God intended labour to be? No. I refuse to let my disappointment lead me into unbelief. Did I experience the fullness of a supernatural childbirth? No; But I will focus on what I did get. My labour was at home, within my time scale and I pushed five times. My baby was healthy and fed so well the midwife was shocked how much weight he put on in the first week. I had torn but I had no grazing and didn't need stitches. I even got my heart's desire: a water birth that hadn't even been on my list! I did have a supernatural childbirth because I saw many things with Heaven's standard. Did I experience the fullness of a supernatural childbirth? No, but I will next time!

✦

15

Nothing ventured nothing gained:
How to deal with disappointment

What happens to our faith when the things we were standing for do not happen? Should we let one experience determine our view of God's character? The way I see it, faith is a choice. I can choose to believe God's Word or not. Even if my experience doesn't line up with the Word I can still choose to believe that God is right, and therefore so is His Word. But how do I get past my disappointment?

If we choose to believe our experience over the words of God, we put our experience in the place of God's Word and that becomes our standard. Our experience becomes an idol because we have placed it above God. We should rather keep the Word of God, God's words, as our standard. If we live by our standard instead of God's we put ourselves in God's place. That can only be dangerous! I would rather throw myself on God, (even if I do not understand the why's and wherefore's), than make my experience my god.

Is it wrong to question when things go wrong? No absolutely not, but let's not allow our reasoning and reliving lead us into a place of unbelief. Did we fail if things don't go according to plan? No, but in some ways yes! There is no condemnation for us (Romans 8:1) and we can start again next time with a clean slate. But I think we need to grow up a little and understand that we have a few reasons before us - either: God is a liar and His Word is not true; the devil is intervening; we need to stand on His Word more efficiently in faith; there may be areas of our mind that are still largely un-renewed and therefore those thought patterns hinder us; or we do not have a full revelation of what is available to us and of who He is. I like to think of it, not as failure or a need for us to work at building more faith, but as a journey of learning. Perhaps we stumble, but we have the ability to pick ourselves back up. Perseverance is key to the journey of faith. We must not be ones who easily give up, but fight the good fight of faith. Proverbs 24:16 says "The godly may trip seven times, but they will get up again. But one disaster is enough to overthrow the wicked." If you are journeying after seeing His Word a reality in the area of walking on water, you make a daily practice of stepping off the side of the pool, fully dressed, believing you will, this time, walk on the surface to the other side. Everyday you fall in, completely soaked through! You may become a little irritated after the one hundredth practice, but you may also laugh, because what you are doing is not 'normal,' it is out of this world's thinking to go after this kind of a breakthrough. It may also be extreme by most Christian thinking, but it is still Biblically available. My point is that in 'extreme faith' the point is perseverance, not failure, the point is to go after it because it's fun, the point is to take these ventures of belief a little less heavily than I have seen many woman default to in believing for a supernatural childbirth. Don't let one failure overthrow your thinking that walking on water is possible, or one failed attempt at a supernatural childbirth, get back up and try again. Falling in the lake each day would not lead you into a place of heavy questioning or spiralling unbelief in who God is and what is available. Sometimes we must show our tenacity and zeal for what we know we can have by continually trying it out until we see it. Our practice of the supernatural becomes a declaration to the spiritual realm that we will go after it until the supernatural becomes a natural way of life. The same is true of any faith venture however tame or extreme you deem them.

I have a choice if I 'fail' or do not see what I was going after. I can either let my experience dictate to my emotions, letting disappointment set in, leading me down a slope of negativity into despair, lowering the standard of God's Word in my life. Or I can let my failures or bad experiences lead me into a determination to overcome next time, to excel in the very area I failed. I turn my greatest failure into my biggest success. We are made as overcomers, we can't be overcomers unless there is something to overcome, even if all we need to overcome is our own un-renewed mind. I believe our enemy wants us to fail, and he gets a kick out of us lying down and letting disappointment crush our faith.

Have you ever had that "Never again" feeling rise up in you, ponder a moment how that made you feel.

However, I also believe that we can kick him in the teeth if we rise up after a disappointment and have a deep resolve that says, "NEVER again!" When we go after the things of God we scare our enemy because he knows the Bible better than we do sometimes. I think he knows that when Christians take their place, with their rightful inheritance they will be unstoppable. Are we really prepared to let the devil get the upper hand because our experience didn't match the words of God this time? Or do we get up and go again until we see it? I choose to get up.

I let the inner peace flood my being, I refresh my mind in the Word and see once again that God is good. I set my face like flint and decide "never again." It's not a bolshie, fisty-cuff faith. It's an inner determination, a tenacity in the depth of ourselves. It comes from a place of rest, a place of security in God's goodness. Every day in creation God looked and saw goodness and then He rested and, I think, pondered this goodness. Let's do the same. Dial down the noise of our lives until only peace remains. Throw off the former thing. Wipe the slate clean. Today is a new day. Speak it aloud over yourself. "Today is a new day." You never know today may be the day that you walk dry to the other side of the pool. Thomas Edison's famous quote puts it so aptly, "many of life's failures are people who did not realise how close they were to success when they gave up."[3]

So what happens if after a bad experience we look back and think we were in faith in the first place? We go back to look over our prayers, quickly analyse our thoughts and the events, and feel that we were in faith. Take it to God, ask Him what happened. Some things I don't understand, nonetheless the thing I do know is God is good and He didn't make me fail. He is still faithful. He still loves me. I am a very pragmatic person and I think we can often deny the obvious. For instance, I was believing for no pain in my second labour yet I experienced pain. I can be stubborn and say I was in faith which implies that it was God who let the side down. Or I can be realistic. I thought I was in faith but obviously I was not because it hurt! I have personally gone over the time leading up to this second labour and tried to think of why it wasn't pain-free. I don't have a complete answer but I have musings. Firstly, when I was typing up the scriptures that had been on 'post its' around the house I noticed that none of them were anything to do with pain or Jesus being my healer. I was not meditating on a pain-free reality. Secondly, I found out after birth that I had had a urine infection for the last few days of my pregnancy. Maybe if I had known, I could have seen this healed and I would therefore not have been in pain during labour. I also had Pelvic Girdle Pain during this pregnancy. I had not been wise enough to tone up properly between pregnancies and my muscles weren't fit enough to endure another pregnancy without stressing. I let myself ask these questions a few days after birth once my emotions settled and I pondered their answers. I would not let my asking lead me down a path of unbelief. I determined not to lower the standard to what I had experienced.

I determined not to lower the standard to what I had experienced

For whatever reason my faith had not worked and I was physically unprepared. However, I resolved with myself that it would next time. Not a desperate resolve but a quiet assurance. I may have lost this battle but I will still win the war.

Are you holding others or God responsible for your 'failure'? Do you need to forgive God? Not that He did anything wrong you understand, but it breaks something in us to forgive God if we are holding it against Him. When we forgive we release that person, even God, from our judgement of them. In our hearts we can hold a person accountable for our situation. If we do that we say that they are to blame; we think in our hearts that they are in the wrong. The person may not have done anything. For example, a child may feel unloved by a parent who works long hours at two different jobs to pay the bills. The parent has done nothing wrong by providing the best they can for the child, and is actually loving the child by providing for them, but the child feels owed love by the parent. In their heart they are holding their parent responsible for not being there. When we hold unforgiveness towards anyone we lock ourselves in prison. We think that the poison of unforgiveness is hurting the other person, when in fact we only hurt ourselves. Unforgiveness makes us bitter and separates us from the Godhead. Do you need to forgive yourself for not standing on the Word? Are you feeling like it was your fault, or that there is something wrong with you for not achieving? Does my suggesting that the failing may have been you, offend you? Get in a quiet place and ask Jesus, "What happened?" "Have I lowered the standard?" "Have I made my experience an idol?" Use your journal pages to help you work through anything that may be holding you back from reaching your idea of a supernatural childbirth next time round. You need to forgive yourself if you are blaming yourself for not seeing the fullness.

Any athlete running a race prepares to win. They train and think positively. But not every runner wins every time and they may not finish within their ideal time if they do. They may stumble. But watching footage of the race will help them improve for their next race. When your emotions have settled a little you need to do some self-appraisal. Look at your race of childbearing. What happened? Look at the stumbles and falls as a way of training for your next childbearing race. I know that next time I'm going to tone up between races so my body will be more able. I know that I'm going

Galatians 5:7 says "You were running a good race. Who cut in on you to keep you from obeying the truth?"

to have more post-its on a pain-free reality. Any good athlete learns how to improve their technique: let's do the same, brushing off the disappointment and going after it again. Galatians 5:7 says "You were running a good race. Who cut in on you to keep you from obeying the truth?" Through disappointment, we can become distracted from going back again and finishing the race that we were robbed of winning because someone, or something cut us off. Yes, it's irritating that it didn't work out perfectly the first time and it may mean that you have those experiences that you need to process, but the truth remains the truth and you were running a good race before you were cut in on, so you can do it again, you're a good runner.

I heard an explanation on a podcast by Bill Johnson,[4] (from Bethel Church in California), that helped me be at peace with my experience. One Kings eighteen tells us there had been a drought in the land for many years, when Elijah got a word from God that rain was on its way. He went up a mountain and started to believe, pray for, and contend for that promise of rain. Each time he finished he sent his servant to look for clouds: each time the servant came back and said that he only saw a cloudless sky. He would pray again with everything within him, with expectation, believing that even though it looked impossible, the next prayer would bring breakthrough to the promise and the rain would begin.

Finally the servant spotted a cloud as small as a man's hand on the horizon - he was not impressed. But it was enough for Elijah. He gathered up his robe and ran to tell the king that heavy rain was coming. He not only ran fast but was gifted supernaturally and he overtook chariots drawn by horses!

Not only in childbirth but in all of life we must get tenacious about the promises God has given us. Jesus has taken the pain in childbirth away. It's a promise because the curse is broken and pain is gone through the power of the cross. We can find many promises in the Word about provision, healing, and everything else. But we need to go after and believe for them until we see them manifest, even if each time we believe, we don't see it. If you've had a bad experience in labour go after it again in your next pregnancy until you see a cloud. People will tell us that pain-free labour is impossible, that it's a cloudless sky. Even our friends, like Elijah's servant, when they see the sign of a small cloud, will not believe because they are not running with the same revelation that we are, the same promise. However, for someone who has heard God, the smallest sign is confirmation. But for someone who doesn't know the promise, like the servant, they will need a larger sign. The small cloud sent Elijah running to tell Ahab to get inside before he was washed away. We need to surround ourselves with people who cheer us on. At my baby shower the second time around, a good friend of mine prayed over me that Heaven and its cloud of witnesses were giving me a standing ovation, spurring me on, "Come on. You can do it Jo." This image filled me with hope, I was known in Heaven, even if no one on earth understood what I was doing. The people who went before me were giving me a standing ovation! They are doing the same for you, "Come on, you can do it". Find people on earth who will join them and help you achieve the fullness of a supernatural childbirth, and all the other promises you are going after.

However, the smallest sign for someone who has the word of God is a confirmation

When we take hold of the promises of God He goes and does immeasurably more than we can ask or hope for (Ephesians 3:20). Believing the promise and the small sign can lead you into greater miracles and breakthrough where you can run faster than the horses.

What is your cloudless sky? What are the promises you have not seen fulfilled? Get tenacious and keep on pressing in until it happens. Don't let your disappointment lead you into unbelief. Run the race with perseverance, get up, brush yourself off and run again, fixing your eyes on Jesus because "His divine power has given us everything we need for a godly life through our knowledge of Him who called us by his own glory and goodness.

Through these He has given us His very great and precious promises, so that through them you may participate in the divine nature, having escaped the corruption in the world caused by evil desires" (2 Peter 1:3-4). It is only as we throw ourselves back on Him in the place of His presence, in the throne room of grace and mercy. The Amplified version says "Through the full personal knowledge of Him". It's from a place of knowing Him personally that we have divine power and grace, then we have divine promises, such as the possibility of a supernatural childbirth. This verse says we can have the divine nature and escape the world's standard. So it's not that we were not in enough faith to receive what we were believing, but that our knowledge of Him needed to be increased and our mind needed further renewal. As He is revealed to us so are His promises over us. To simply read the concept of a supernatural standard in childbirth without revelation of the One who made it possible is not enough to succeed. The principles do work, but confession of those principles alone can become a crutch. He needs to be the one we lean in to. Every birth needs to come from a now revelation, out of a place of relationship, we need to receive fresh manna from Heaven for this time round. The Israelites were disappointed with the desert and complained a lot but God was still faithful to them, raining down on them all manna from Heaven and meeting all their needs. If you have had a previous bad experience of birth, no matter how disgruntled you feel, God is still faithful. This birth can be different from your last one. I don't think it is wrong to feel disappointment but be careful that your disappointment doesn't lead you into complaints and grumblings. You will very quickly slip into unbelief, just as the Israelites did. The aim is to reach the promised land immediately, without complaint. "We do not want you to become lazy, but to imitate those who through faith and patience inherit what has been promised" (Hebrew 6:12).

✦

16

In Father's arms:

Following on from how to deal with disappointment I wanted to touch briefly on miscarriage. For those of you that have had a miscarriage I am truly sorry for your loss. Losing a child, even at an underdeveloped stage is painful. Miscarriage is a really tragic thing.

People respond very differently to miscarriage. Some people shrug and seem to move on very quickly, but for others it can be a very painful and lengthy process, as they come to terms with what has happened. I think it can be more painful when you are believing for the supernatural and then something like this comes along. It is difficult to have been standing on scripture and praying, lose a baby and then go back into a place of believing again. It is very hard not to spiral into a place of disappointment. Once you have had one miscarriage it can be a difficult battle with fear when you think about becoming, or have become pregnant again. Once again it comes down to the battlefield of your mind and guarding your heart from fear of a repeat experience.

I cannot say anything that will help you. All that anyone can say is that they are sorry and that just does not cut it. It is in Him that you need to find your comfort, in Him that you will find strength. Take time if you need it and allow Him to comfort you. You do not have to try and work it all out. You do not need to put on a brave face, you are free to ask, cry, scream and rant with God; He is not afraid of your emotion, it's better out than in. With Him is a safe space to let your true feelings free. Let Him woo you to Himself. It's a process. Processes can take time and that is okay. When you are ready, get a trusted friend to pray with you. Talk to people you can trust and work through what you are feeling.

Disappointment is an enemy of faith. Do not let your questioning lead to unbelief. God wants you to have children (Deuteronomy 7:14), despite what your past experiences may have left you thinking. The devil is out to kill, steal and destroy (John 10:10), God by His nature can do none of these things. God did not take your baby, He is not punishing you, He poured all His wrath on Jesus on the cross at Calvary. He is not trying to teach you something, God is not a mean father but one of love. Taking a child from someone is not a loving act, it is an act of the enemy. Miscarriage is a robbery. Still, I have good news, God gives back seven times what is stolen from you (Proverbs 6:31). You may not want seven children! But the principle is the same, God wants to bless you with more than what was taken from you. He wants your quiver full of children (Psalm 127:4-5).

Disappointment is an enemy of faith. Do not let your questioning lead to unbelief.

When you lose a child you need to grieve. In English culture especially, grief is not something that we do well but grieving is healthy. Something precious has been taken from you. It's a loss; it will take time to process and to heal. Tears are healthy, a broken heart is not. Firstly, God wants you whole. Throw yourself back on Holy Spirit, the comforter. Don't be afraid to let loose your anguish to God. However if you believe that God was the one that allowed your baby to be taken from you, or if you think that He took the baby Himself to punish or teach you, then how can you grieve? If it was God's will (which it was not), then we must resign ourselves to the fact that we must accept His will for us, even though it hurts.

Grief cannot truly be realised if you battle between "it was God who did this" versus the emotion of loss that wants to envelop you. If you believe it was God then your relationship with Him will ultimately suffer. You can never build trust with someone who would steal from you.

I believe that God is a life giver. No matter the circumstances leading up to a miscarriage I believe that God's intention is for every baby to live. God is into healing and raising the dead and has commissioned us with the authority to do the same (Mark 16:15-18). I have heard of a few stories where babies have died in the womb and when the women have been prayed for their babies jump back to life again. My brother-in-law started talking with a pregnant lady who was homeless, she had not felt the baby move for days and was at a loss of what to do. When he prayed the baby immediately started to kick. God is the God who does the impossible. It is never too late to believe for a miracle. I was sent another great testimony recently that I thought was appropriate to include here:

Grief can not truly be realised if you battle between "it was God who did this" verses the emotion of loss that wants to envelop you

"*I was pregnant with my second child. Whilst on holiday abroad with my husband and fifteen month old daughter I started to experience severe cramping. About half an hour after the cramping started I had a bleed. At the time I believed myself to be about seven to eight weeks pregnant, although I wasn't exactly sure of my dates.*

I remember standing in the public toilet cubicle having just discovered I was bleeding, feeling a mixture of fear, sadness, shock and anger at the sight of the blood. In that moment I recalled how I had set out in this pregnancy declaring the plans and purposes of God over the baby and myself. So in that moment I spoke life over my baby. I think out of shear anger with the enemy I said out loud "I refuse to miscarry".

My husband and I commanded the pain and bleeding to stop. The bleeding stopped immediately and the pain within twenty minutes of praying.

We wanted to go to the hospital to have everything checked out and be sure it was ok for me to fly home the next day. Finding a hospital was easier said than done as we were abroad and we had quite literally nearly run out of money. We couldn't afford the English speaking private American hospital as I needed a scan and this is pricey! So we ended up at the local public hospital. The doctor we were assigned to perform the scan understandably did not speak English but also sadly was very lacking in people skills and sensitivity. During the scan the yoke sac was located but no heart beat was present, I knew that either we had the dates wrong and it was in fact too early to see a heartbeat (you would definitely expect to see one by seven to eight weeks) or our baby was not alive.

The doctor was very abrupt and insensitive with us and made no attempts to explain the scan. The language barrier meant that our questions remained unanswered. I left that hospital feeling more fearful and bemused than when I went in.

The period of time between this scan and waiting for our twelve week routine scan felt like decades and was an incredibly challenging few weeks with regards to my faith. We made the decision to declare life over our little baby and stand on the promises of God for his plans and purposes to prevail in this pregnancy. During this time however I constantly battled with thoughts of delayed miscarriage and bad news. When my twelve week scan came we were told our baby was healthy and well and I was in fact a little earlier than I thought I was.

It may then have been completely normal that the heartbeat wasn't visible in this early scan or it may have been that Jesus supernaturally intervened to bring life where there was none. Either way that period of unknown taught me a lot about standing on the promises of God for my baby and myself. To cling to Jesus and only let Him whisper in my ears in times of uncertainty where the enemy tries to plant fear. God has plans to prosper us and not to harm us. Plans to give us hope and a future!"

So if you start to bleed find His peace, get tenacious. Go to the doctor, if you get a bad report find that peace, get tenacious. Find people of faith to stand with you. I went through this experience with my third pregnancy, I had just found out I was pregnant, but was only showing a faint positive line on the test, but I was far enough overdue with my period that I was certain I was pregnant although I was having period cramps. I started to tell a few people that I was pregnant but the next day I started to bleed, I wasn't worried at first as I had had spot bleeding in my other pregnancies, but I prayed life over my baby anyway and carried on with my day. However the cramps continued and by the afternoon I was bleeding heavily. I remembered the story of King David in the Bible when he was praying for his baby to live, he wept and fasted and did everything in his power to keep the baby alive. The baby died. David got up, stopped mourning and went on to have many children with Bathsheba, including Solomon, who Jesus descended from. After a three day faith fight I lost my baby. It was such a quick turn around of emotions I felt a little numb. I was five weeks and two days pregnant when I miscarried. After I stopped bleeding I processed with God. I asked Jesus to comfort me and I cried. I was sad. Mourning is good and proper, and for those of you who have lost a baby - I mourn with you. However, there does come a time when we need to take a deep breath, draw a line in the sand and move into the promises of God. He has promised children. You will be victorious. There is no condemnation, you are not the cause of the miscarriage, you did not lose your baby, it is not your fault. You may never know why it happened, but I assure you God didn't want you to lose your baby either. Right now your baby is living a glorious existence in Heaven, they have the best father caring for them and one day you will see them again. Your body may have miscarried your baby but your baby is now carried in the arms of our loving father. He has your baby in a loving embrace and has carried them to Heaven to await your arrival.

The same is true for those who have had abortions. Your baby is safe and loved. God Himself now has your child. They are happy together, playing and running in the never ending warmth of love. You need to forgive yourself and let God minister His forgiveness to you. This issue is not too large for Him to take away. He will restore your peace and joy when you think of your lost child. He will take away the barb the experience has left in your heart. I am not saying you will forget, but that you will be able to think about it without pain. God loves us in spite of our history, He paid the price for the bad and wants us to live free from its consequences.

Every experience has a way of teaching us things, about ourselves and about God. Your past has bearing on who you are now, but you have a choice not to let your past hold you back from living in the fullness of what is available to you now. God has wiped the slate clean - are you prepared to do the same for yourself? You must stop holding yourself to account for you past and let God close enough to heal your heart. You are not beyond love and it is His to give to whomever He chooses.

A friend of mine wrote her unborn child a letter and it really helped her in her healing process. Why don't you do the same?

✦

17

Oil in my lamp:

How to burn after birth

In my first pregnancy I was so focused on my coming labour that I forgot that I still needed to live supernaturally after birth! I had a fantastic experience at delivery but was totally unprepared for being a supernatural Mum! I was so preoccupied with the birth I had forgotten the end goal - a baby!

During pregnancy there seems to be so much to think about: work, your changing body, maternity leave, baby equipment, choosing a name, decorating, shopping, hospital appointments and the birth. Somewhere in there you need to make time to prepare yourself for motherhood. Just as you have prepared with scriptures for birth, I think it is a good idea to have an after birth post-it pile prepared! When you remove your scriptures for labour, you then have a pile ready to stick up to help maintain a focus on supernatural living. It is easy to slip from the standard you have now set by determining to have a supernatural childbirth. You have raised the bar in your life and it is for you to maintain. All the

Let the tenacity you have learned to walk in take over and go after supernatural living in every area.

principles you have read in the previous chapters are not just for your pregnancy, but for your life after birth. After delivery, God is still interested in you living from heavenly places and has made a way for you to do so every day.

I think it is important to research parenting styles. Routines verses baby lead: dummy or none: formula or breast fed and all the other questions surrounding how you want to raise your child. Information is good. You need to make these decisions while you're pregnant rather than when your child is screaming at three o'clock in the morning and you realise you are in fact pro dummies! Sometimes our plans are foiled. Flexibility is the key to parenting without stress or over-worry. We had friends who planned to use washable nappies; they were adamant that not one disposable nappy would ever be used. Three months later, although they were still fairly eco-friendly, disposables were on the shopping list!

I think as parents you are responsible for your child on many levels. The Bible tells us to train a child in the way they should go and they will walk in it (Proverbs 22:6). You can train them practically to sleep through the night, to talk and walk, but what about their spiritual training? Spiritual training starts at an early age and even if you don't think you are doing it, you are! Behaviour is mimicked and picked up, it is learnt by observing. Put into practice what you want your children to learn. If you cultivate an atmosphere of Kingdom in your home, your child will grow up in a secure environment and become a Kingdom person themselves. You have already started to do this. By immersing yourself in His presence you are also encasing your baby with the presence. Every day of pregnancy your baby can be saturated with an atmosphere of Heaven. As you choose to cultivate an environment where you become conscious of His presence, you are overshadowed by it and so is your unborn child. Even in these nine months you are setting them up for life, a life spent in the presence of God. Simply because of the environment you create you are marking your child with the Glory of God. What an amazing starting point! Samuel as a boy spent his nights sleeping in God's presence. He was the only one in his day who was hearing God speak, it is no coincidence that he grew up in the presence (1 Samuel 3:3). From being in the presence, verse nineteen says "the Lord was with Samuel as he grew up, and he let none of his words fall to the ground". What a promise that our babies can live in as we create this place of His presence in our lives. After birth, let's continue to cultivate this same atmosphere in our homes where the supernatural life becomes standard living practice. Put soaking music or podcasts on during breastfeeding. Have scripture post-its around. Take authority in the spirit and see your child live free from sickness, trapped wind, colic, sleepless nights and other 'normal' things for newborns. Who says you should be tired all the time? Who says you should have baby blues and mood swings after birth? Medical thinking says that as your uterus retracts after birth it should be a painful experience. It is often said that after your third and fourth child this contracting back to size is more painful than labour. That doesn't sound like 'normal' to me. These principles are for more than pregnancy, labour and newborns. There is no reason we should be believing for the terrible twos, troublesome threes, and rebellious teens. I don't believe that is God's standard. Let the tenacity you have learned to walk in take over and go after supernatural living in every area. I was unaware of how unprepared I was and overwhelmed when I realised! I was tired and teary in my first few weeks as a first

Make a list while your pregnant of what you think 'normal' heavenly standard living looks like for you and your new born.

time mum and I didn't need to be. Fill the oil in your lamp (Matthew 25) prior to delivery, so that amongst the busy first few months of having a newborn you can draw from the well within you (Isaiah 12:3). It is not that you cannot spend time with God when you have children, but it is different and sometimes difficult to schedule quality time. Get the quality time now so that you are starting motherhood with a 'topped up' spirit. After birth you can cultivate spontaneous prayer and an awareness of Him being with you in the every day moments. Both things are important for a relationship to be strong: sharing life and sharing quality intimate time. But the Bible says in Isaiah 40:11, that "He gently leads those who have young," He is not expectant of you in any way. He will lead you along with Himself and you will never miss out on anything just because you are a mother.

Practically, if you are able, make sure you are still having time for you. Schedule in time for your husband or mother to have the kids. Go to the movies, a coffee, to a friends, or go for a hot bubble bath (with the door locked!) To maintain this new supernatural platform we need to be grounded in the natural, your body needs to rest just as much as your spirit and soul. My advice is, in order for you to keep living at this new level of faith, fill up with Him, fill up rest, fill up going out now so that you are ready. This is something I did not do!

In my second pregnancy I got prepared. I was tenacious in my soul, and peaceful in my spirit for labour, for a baby, but I forgot my body. God has made us whole people. Body, spirit and soul. We are to be Kingdom people in all three areas, no one thing is better or worse than the other, but all three should work harmoniously with each other, just like the trinity. We are reflections of God, made in His image. My kids are twenty months apart, between having my first and falling pregnant with my second, I did nothing to help my body recover. I didn't think I needed to, I felt fine. I have never been a sporty person and am very lacking in self discipline when it comes to exercise! I fit quickly back into my old clothes and for me that was enough. How wrong I was! When my second baby started to grow so that I had a reasonable sized bump I had tremendous pain in my hip. My midwife referred me to Physiotherapy and I was diagnosed with Pelvic Girdle Pain. I ended up having to wear a supportive belt because my muscles weren't doing their job. A year after delivery I was doing Pilates to help correct the damage I had done by not toning up between pregnancies. I cannot stress enough how equally important each area of our being is. I made a decision that the next time I intend to be fully ready, spirit, soul and body.

I have always been one to take God at His word, but during my pregnancies I have grown dynamically in my tenacity to see His Word become real in my life on a really practical level. I have learnt from all these experiences and have turned my mistakes into lessons for the future. These lessons have leaked through to all avenues of my life and marked me to be a supernaturally minded believer. Viewing childbirth from a biblical perspective is no different from how we should be viewing the rest of life, from the same biblical perspective. We are all on a journey of mind renewal to a heavenly sonship perspective and for me my childbearing experiences have accelerated that process and grounded teaching that before was simply theory.

✦

18

Scriptural Blueprints:
His Word and reality manifest in you

Below are some of the scriptures I used to pray and speak over my body so that it would come in line with the Word of God. (You will find these scriptures throughout your journal also). Having experiences of God is an awesome way to know Him but His Word gives us a beautiful tapestry of His character and gives us a grounding for our experiences.

Scriptures about joy:

Deuteronomy 16:15 ...For the LORD your God will bless you in all your harvest and in all the work of your hands, and your joy will be complete.

Nehemiah 8:10 ...for the joy of the LORD is your strength.

Psalm 16:6-13 The boundary lines have fallen for me in pleasant places; surely I have a delightful inheritance. I will praise the LORD, who counsels me; even at night my heart instructs me. I keep my eyes always on the LORD. With him at my right hand, I will not be shaken. Therefore my heart is glad and my tongue rejoices; my body also will rest secure, because you will not abandon me to the realm of the dead, nor will you let your faithful one see decay. You make known to me the path of life; you will fill me with joy in your presence, with eternal pleasures at your right hand.

Psalm 37:4 Delight yourself in the LORD and he will give you the desires of your heart.

Psalm 103:1-5 Praise the LORD, my soul; all my inmost being, praise his holy name. Praise the LORD, my soul, and forget not all his benefits—who forgives all your sins and heals all your diseases, who redeems your life from the pit and crowns you with love and compassion, who satisfies your desires with good things so that your youth is renewed like the eagle's.

Psalm 119:23-24 Though rulers sit together and slander me, your servant will meditate on your decrees. Your statutes are my delight; they are my counsellors.

Psalm 126: 1-3 When the LORD restored the fortunes of Zion, we were like those who dreamed. Our mouths were filled with laughter, our tongues with songs of joy. Then it was said among the nations, "The LORD has done great things for them." The LORD has done great things for us, and we are filled with joy.

Psalm 126:5-6 Those who sow with tears will reap with songs of joy. Those who go out weeping, carrying seed to sow, will return with songs of joy, carrying sheaves with them.

Proverbs 17.22 A cheerful heart is good medicine, but a crushed spirit dries up the bones.

Proverbs 18:20-21 From the fruit of their mouth a person's stomach is filled; with the harvest of their lips they are satisfied. The tongue has the power of life and death, and those who love it will eat its fruit.

Proverbs 23:7 (NKJ) For as he thinks in his heart, so is he.

Proverbs 23:25 May your father and mother rejoice; may she who gave you birth be joyful!

Isaiah 61:3 and provide for those who grieve in Zion to bestow on them a crown of beauty instead of ashes, the oil of joy instead of mourning, and a garment of praise instead of a spirit of despair. They will be called oaks of righteousness, a planting of the LORD for the display of His splendour.

Romans 12:12 Be joyful in hope, patient in affliction, faithful in prayer.

Romans 15:13 May the God of hope fill you with all joy and peace as you trust in Him, so that you may overflow with hope by the power of the Holy Spirit.

2 Corinthians 8:2 In the midst of a very severe trial, their overflowing joy and their extreme poverty welled up in rich generosity.

Colossians 1:10-12 So that you may live a life worthy of the Lord and please him in every way: bearing fruit in every good work, growing in the knowledge of God, being strengthened with all power according to His glorious might so that you may have great endurance and patience, and giving joyful thanks to the Father, who has qualified you to share in the inheritance of His holy people in the kingdom of light.

Hebrews 1.9 ...therefore God, your God, has set you above your companions by anointing you with the oil of joy.

James 1:2 Consider it pure joy, my brothers and sisters, whenever you face trials of many kinds.

Scriptures about barrenness and miscarriage:

Deuteronomy 7:13 He will love you and bless you and increase your numbers. He will bless the fruit of your womb, the crops of your land—your grain, new wine and olive oil—the calves of your herds and the lambs of your flocks in the land he swore to your ancestors to give you.

1 Samuel 1:27 I prayed for this child, and the LORD has granted me what I asked of him.

Psalm 71: 2-8 In your righteousness, rescue me and deliver me; turn your ear to me and save me. Be my rock of refuge, to which I can always go; give the command to save me, for you are my rock and my fortress. Deliver me, my God, from the hand of the wicked, from the grasp of those who are evil and cruel. For you have been my hope, Sovereign LORD, my confidence since my youth. From birth I have relied on you; you brought me forth from my mother's womb. I will ever praise you. I have become a sign to many; you are my strong refuge. My mouth is filled with your praise, declaring your splendour all day long.

Psalm 128:1-3 Blessed are all who fear the LORD, who walk in obedience to him. You will eat the fruit of your labour; blessings and prosperity will be yours. Your wife will be like a fruitful vine within your house; your children will be like olive shoots around your table.

Psalm 139:13-19 For you created my inmost being; you knit me together in my mother's womb. I praise you because I am fearfully and wonderfully made; your works are wonderful, I know that full well. My frame was not hidden from you when I was made in the secret place, when I was woven together in the depths of the earth. Your eyes saw my unformed body; all the days ordained for me were written in your book before one of them came to be. How precious to me are your thoughts, God! How vast is the sum of them! Were I to count them, they would outnumber the grains of sand when I awake, I am still with you. If only you, God, would slay the wicked! Away from me, you who are bloodthirsty!

Jeremiah 1:5 "Before I formed you in the womb I knew you, before you were born I set you apart; I appointed you as a prophet to the nations."

Malachi 3:10-11 Bring the whole tithe into the storehouse, that there may be food in my house. Test me in this," says the LORD Almighty, "and see if I will not throw open the floodgates of Heaven and pour out so much blessing that you will not have room enough for it. I will prevent pests from devouring your crops, and the vines in your fields will not cast their fruit," says the LORD Almighty.

Romans 4:18-21 Against all hope, Abraham in hope believed and so became the father of many nations, just as it had been said to him, "So shall your offspring be." Without weakening in his faith, he faced the fact that his body was as good as dead—since he was about a hundred years old—and that Sarah's womb was also dead. Yet he did not waver through unbelief regarding the promise of God, but was strengthened in his faith and gave glory to God, being fully persuaded that God had power to do what he had promised.

Scriptures about fear:

1 Samuel 30:6 David was greatly distressed, for the men spoke of stoning him because the souls of them all were bitterly grieved, each man for his sons and daughters. But David encouraged and strengthened himself in the Lord his God.

Psalm 34:4 I sought the LORD, and He answered me; He delivered me from all my fears.

Proverbs 17:20 One whose heart is corrupt does not prosper; one whose tongue is perverse falls into trouble.

Proverbs 18:20-21 From the fruit of their mouth a person's stomach is filled; with the harvest of their lips they are satisfied. The tongue has the power of life and death, and those who love it will eat its fruit.

Isaiah 41:10 Fear not, for I am with you; Be not dismayed, for I am your God. I will strengthen you, yes, I will help you, I will uphold you with My righteous right hand.'

Jeremiah 42:16 Then the sword you fear will overtake you there, and the famine you dread will follow you into Egypt, and there you will die.

Matthew 6:31-33 So do not worry, saying, 'What shall we eat?' or 'What shall we drink?' or 'What shall we wear?' For the pagans run after all these things, and your heavenly Father knows that you need them. But seek first his kingdom and his righteousness, and all these things will be given to you as well.

2 Corinthians 10:5 We demolish arguments and every pretension that sets itself up against the knowledge of God, and we take captive every thought to make it obedient to Christ.

2 Timothy 1:7 For God has not given us a spirit of fear, but of power and of love and of a sound mind.

Hebrews 11:1 Now faith is confidence in what we hope for and assurance about what we do not see.

1 John 4:18 There is no fear in love [dread does not exist], but full-grown (complete, perfect) love turns fear out of doors and expels every trace of terror! For fear brings with it the thought of punishment, and [so] he who is afraid has not reached the full maturity of love [is not yet grown into love's complete perfection].

Scriptures about trust and rest:

2 Chronicles 6:40-42 "Now, my God, may your eyes be open and your ears attentive to the prayers offered in this place. "Now arise,

LORD God, and come to your resting place, you and the ark of your might. May your priests, LORD God, be clothed with salvation, may your faithful people rejoice in your goodness. LORD God, do not reject your anointed one. Remember the great love promised to David your servant."

Psalm 16:8-10 I keep my eyes always on the LORD. With him at my right hand, I will not be shaken. Therefore my heart is glad and my tongue rejoices; my body also will rest secure.

Psalm 22:9 Yet you brought me out of the womb; you made me trust in you, even at my mother's breast.

Psalm 23:1-6 The LORD is my shepherd, I lack nothing. He makes me lie down in green pastures, he leads me beside quiet waters, he refreshes my soul. He guides me along the right paths for his name's sake. Even though I walk through the darkest valley, I will fear no evil, for you are with me; your rod and your staff, they comfort me. You prepare a table before me in the presence of my enemies. You anoint my head with oil; my cup overflows. Surely your goodness and love will follow me all the days of my life, and I will dwell in the house of the LORD forever.

Psalm 32:8 I will instruct you and teach you in the way you should go; I will counsel you with my loving eye on you.

Psalm 36:7-9 How priceless is your unfailing love, O God! People take refuge in the shadow of your wings. They feast on the abundance of your house; you give them drink from your river of delights. For with you is the fountain of life; in your light we see light.

Psalm 37:4 Delight yourself in the LORD and he will give you the desires of your heart.

Psalm 62:1-2 Truly my soul finds rest in God; my salvation comes from him. Truly he is my rock and my salvation; he is my fortress, I will never be shaken.

Psalm 91:1-4 Whoever dwells in the shelter of the Most High will rest in the shadow of the Almighty. I will say of the LORD, "He is my refuge and my fortress, my God, in whom I trust." Surely he will save you from the fowler's snare and from the deadly pestilence. He will cover you with his feathers, and under his wings you will find refuge; his faithfulness will be your shield and rampart.

Psalm 139:17-18 How precious to me are your thoughts God! How vast is the sum of them! Were I to count them, they would outnumber the grains of sand— when I awake, I am still with you.

Isaiah 30:21 Whether you turn to the right or to the left, your ears will hear a voice behind you, saying, "This is the way; walk in it."

Jeremiah 29:11-13 For I know the plans I have for you," declares the LORD, "plans to prosper you and not to harm you, plans to give you hope and a future. Then you will call on me and come and pray to me, and I will listen to you. You will seek me and find me when you seek me with all your heart.

Lamentations 3:22-24 Because of the Lord's great love we are not consumed, for his compassions never fail. They are new every morning; great is your faithfulness. I say to myself, "The LORD is my portion; therefore I will wait for him."

Zechariah 12:8-9 On that day the LORD will shield those who live in Jerusalem, so that the feeblest among them will be like David, and the house of David will be like God, like the angel of the LORD going before them. On that day I will set out to destroy all the nations that attack Jerusalem.

Matthew 25:1-3 At that time the kingdom of Heaven will be like ten virgins who took their lamps and went out to meet the bridegroom. Five of them were foolish and five were wise. The foolish ones took their lamps but did not take any oil with them.

Luke 1:37 For nothing is impossible with God.

John 14:2-4 My Father's house has many rooms; if that were not so, would I have told you that I am going there to prepare a place for you? And if I go and prepare a place for you, I will come back and take you to be with me that you also may be where I am. You know the way to the place where I am going."

John 15:4 Abide in Me, and I in you. As the branch cannot bear fruit of itself, unless it abides in the vine, neither can you, unless you abide in Me.

John 15:7 If you abide in Me, and My words abide in you, you will ask what you desire, and it shall be done for you.

Romans 15:13 May the God of hope fill you with all joy and peace as you trust in him, so that you may overflow with hope by the power of the Holy Spirit."

2 Corinthians 12:9-10 But he said to me, "My grace is sufficient for you, for my power is made perfect in weakness." Therefore I will boast all the more gladly about my weaknesses, so that Christ's power may rest on me. That is why, for Christ's sake, I delight in weaknesses, in insults, in hardships, in persecutions, in difficulties. For when I am weak, then I am strong.

Philippians 4:11-13 I am not saying this because I am in need, for I have learned to be content whatever the circumstances. I know what it is to be in need, and I know what it is to have plenty. I have learned the secret of being content in any and every situation, whether well fed or hungry, whether living in plenty or in want. I can do all this through him who gives me strength.

Hebrew 4: 9 There remains, then, a Sabbath-rest for the people of God; for anyone who enters God's rest also rests from their works, just as God did from his. Let us, therefore, make every effort to enter that rest, so that no one will perish by following their example of disobedience.

Scriptures about your baby's growth:

Genesis 1:27 So God created mankind in his own image, in the image of God he created them; male and female he created them.

Deuteronomy 28:11 The LORD will grant you abundant prosperity in the fruit of your womb...

Joshua 24:15 But as for me and my household, we will serve the LORD.

Job 8:7 Though your beginning was small, Yet your latter end would increase abundantly.

Psalm 22:9 Yet you brought me out of the womb; you made me trust in you, even at my mother's breast. From birth I was cast on you; from my mother's womb you have been my God.

Psalm 51:6 Yet you desired faithfulness even in the womb; you taught me wisdom in that secret place.

Psalm 71:5-8 For you have been my hope, Sovereign LORD, my confidence since my youth. From birth I have relied on you; you brought me forth from my mother's womb. I will ever praise you. I have become a sign to many; you are my strong refuge. My mouth is filled with your praise, declaring your splendour all day long.

Psalm 103:17 But from everlasting to everlasting the Lord's love is with those who fear him, and his righteousness with their children's children.

Psalm 139:13-19 For you created my inmost being; you knit me together in my mother's womb. I praise you because I am fearfully and wonderfully made; your works are wonderful, I know that full well. My frame was not hidden from you when I was made in the secret place, when I was woven together in the depths of the earth. Your eyes saw my unformed body; all the days ordained for me were written in your book before one of them came to be. How precious to me are your thoughts, God! How vast is the sum of them! Were I to count them, they would outnumber the grains of sand when I awake, I am still with you. If only you, God, would slay the wicked! Away from me, you who are bloodthirsty!

Proverbs 22:6 Start children off on the way they should go, and even when they are old they will not turn from it.

Isaiah 38:19 The living, the living—they praise you, as I am doing today; parents tell their children about your faithfulness.

Isaiah 44:3 For I will pour out water to quench your thirst and to irrigate your parched fields. And I will pour out my Spirit on your descendants, and my blessing on your children.

Isaiah 49:1 Before I was born the LORD called me; from my mother's womb he has spoken my name.

Isaiah 66:9 Do I bring to the moment of birth and not give delivery?" says the LORD. "Do I close up the womb when I bring to delivery?" says your God.

Jeremiah 1:4-7 The word of the LORD came to me, saying, "Before I formed you in the womb I knew you, before you were born I set you apart; I appointed you as a prophet to the nations." "Alas, Sovereign LORD," I said, "I do not know how to speak; I am too young." But the LORD said to me, "Do not say, 'I am too young.' You must go to everyone I send you to and say whatever I command you.

Jeremiah 29:11 "For I know the plans I have for you," declares the LORD, "plans to prosper you and not to harm you, plans to give you hope and a future."

Luke 1.42 In a loud voice she exclaimed: "Blessed are you among women, and blessed is the child you will bear!

Scriptures about faith and prayer:

Deuteronomy 26:9-11 He brought us to this place and gave us this land, a land flowing with milk and honey; and now I bring the first fruits of the soil that you, LORD, have given me." Place the basket before the LORD your God and bow down before him. Then you and the Levites and the foreigners residing among you shall rejoice in all the good things the LORD your God has given to you and your household.

Joshua 1:8 Do not let this Book of the Law depart from your mouth; meditate on it day and night, so that you may be careful to do everything written in it. Then you will be prosperous and successful.

Psalm 1:1-3 Blessed is the one who does not walk in step with the wicked or stand in the way that sinners take or sit in the company of mockers, but whose delight is in the law of the LORD, and who meditates on his law day and night. That person is like a tree planted by streams of water, which yields its fruit in season and whose leaf does not wither whatever they do prospers.

Psalm 37:4 Delight yourself also in the LORD, and He shall give you the desires of your heart.

Psalm 77:11-13 I will remember the deeds of the LORD; yes, I will remember your miracles of long ago. I will consider all your works and meditate on all your mighty deeds." Your ways, God, are holy. What god is as great as our God?

Proverbs 25:2 It is the glory of God to conceal a matter; to search out a matter is the glory of kings.

Ecclesiastes 3:1 There is a time for everything, and a season for every activity under the heavens.

Isaiah 38:1-7 In those days Hezekiah became ill and was at the point of death. The prophet Isaiah son of Amoz went to him and said, "This is what the LORD says: Put your house in order, because you are going to die; you will not recover." Hezekiah turned his face to the wall and prayed to the LORD, "Remember, LORD, how I have walked before you faithfully and with wholehearted devotion and have done what is good in your eyes." And Hezekiah wept bitterly. Then the word of the LORD came to Isaiah: "Go and tell Hezekiah, 'This is what the LORD, the God of your father David, says: I have heard your prayer and seen your tears; I will add fifteen years to your life. And I will deliver you and this city from the hand of the king of Assyria. I will defend this city. This is the Lord's sign to you that the LORD will do what he has promised.

Isaiah 40:31 But those who hope in the LORD will renew their strength. They will soar on wings like eagles; they will run and not grow weary, they will walk and not be faint.

Jeremiah 1:12 The LORD said to me, "You have seen correctly, for I am watching to see that my word is fulfilled."

Habakkuk 2:3 For the revelation awaits an appointed time; it speaks of the end and will not prove false. Though it linger, wait for it; it will certainly come and will not delay.

Matthew 6:5-8 "And when you pray, do not be like the hypocrites, for they love to pray standing in the synagogues and on the street corners to be seen by others. Truly I tell you, they have received their reward in full. But when you pray, go into your room, close the door and pray to your Father, who is unseen. Then your Father, who sees what is done in secret, will reward you. And when you pray, do not keep on babbling like pagans, for they think they will be heard because of their many words. Do not be like them, for your Father knows what you need before you ask him.

Matthew 10:27 What I tell you in the dark, speak in the daylight; what is whispered in your ear, proclaim from the roofs.

Matthew 11:12 And from the days of John the Baptist until the present time, the kingdom of Heaven has endured violent assault, and violent men seize it by force [as a precious prize--a share in the heavenly kingdom is sought with most ardent zeal and intense exertion].

Matthew 18:19-20 Again I tell you, if two of you on earth agree (harmonise together, make a symphony together) about whatever [anything and everything] they may ask, it will come to pass and be done for them by My Father in Heaven. For wherever two or three are gathered (drawn together as My followers) in (into) My name, there I AM in the midst of them.

Matthew 21:21-22 Jesus replied, "Truly I tell you, if you have faith and do not doubt, not only can you do what was done to the fig tree, but also you can say to this mountain, 'Go, throw yourself into the sea,' and it will be done. If you believe, you will receive whatever you ask for in prayer."

Mark 11:22-24 "Have faith in God," Jesus answered. "Truly I tell you, if anyone says to this mountain, 'Go, throw yourself into the sea,' and does not doubt in their heart but believes that what they say will happen, it will be done for them. Therefore I tell you, whatever you ask for in prayer, believe that you have received it, and it will be yours.

Luke 2:19 But Mary treasured up all these things and pondered them in her heart.

Luke 6:45 A good man brings good things out of the good stored up in his heart, and an evil man brings evil things out of the evil stored up in his heart. For the mouth speaks what the heart is full of.

John 16:24 Until now you have not asked for anything in my name. Ask and you will receive, and your joy will be complete.

Romans 8:37-39 No, in all these things we are more than conquerors through him who loved us. For I am convinced that neither death nor life, neither angels nor demons, neither the present nor the future, nor any powers, neither height nor depth, nor anything else in all creation, will be able to separate us from the love of God that is in Christ Jesus our Lord.

Romans 12:2 Do not conform to the pattern of this world, but be transformed by the renewing of your mind. Then you will be able to test and approve what God's will is—his good, pleasing and perfect will.

Romans 15:5-6 May the God who gives endurance and encouragement give you the same attitude of mind toward each other that Christ Jesus had, so that with one mind and one voice you may glorify the God and Father of our Lord Jesus Christ.

1 Corinthians 1:8-9 He will also keep you firm to the end, so that you will be blameless on the day of our Lord Jesus Christ. God is faithful, who has called you into fellowship with his Son, Jesus Christ our Lord.

1 Corinthians 2:16 for, "Who has known the mind of the Lord so as to instruct him?" But we have the mind of Christ.

2 Corinthians 1:20-22 For no matter how many promises God has made, they are "Yes" in Christ. And so through him the "Amen" is spoken by us to the glory of God. Now it is God who makes both us and you stand firm in Christ. He anointed us, set his seal of ownership on us, and put his Spirit in our hearts as a deposit, guaranteeing what is to come.

Ephesians 3:20 Now to him who is able to do immeasurably more than all we ask or imagine, according to his power that is at work within us.

Ephesians 6:13 Therefore put on the full armour of God, so that when the day of evil comes, you may be able to stand your ground, and after you have done everything, to stand.

Philippians 1:6 Being confident of this, that he who began a good work in you will carry it on to completion until the day of Christ Jesus.

Philippians 4:8 Finally, brethren, whatever things are true, whatever things are noble, whatever things are just, whatever things are pure, whatever things are lovely, whatever things are of good report, if there is any virtue and if there is anything praiseworthy—meditate on these things.

Philippians 4:13 I can do everything through him who gives me strength.

Colossians 1:11-12 Being strengthened with all power according to his glorious might so that you may have great endurance and patience, and giving joyful thanks to the Father, who has qualified you to share in the inheritance of his holy people in the kingdom of light.

Colossians 2:6-7 So then, just as you received Christ Jesus as Lord, continue to live your lives in him, rooted and built up in him, strengthened in the faith as you were taught, and overflowing with thankfulness.

1 Thessalonians 1:3-5 We remember before our God and Father your work produced by faith, your labour prompted by love, and your endurance inspired by hope in our Lord Jesus Christ. For we know, brothers and sisters loved by God, that he has chosen you, because our gospel came to you not simply with words but also with power, with the Holy Spirit and deep conviction.

2 Thessalonians 2:16-17 May our Lord Jesus Christ himself and God our Father, who loved us and by his grace gave us eternal encouragement and good hope, encourage your hearts and strengthen you in every good deed and word.

2 Timothy 1:7 For the Spirit God gave us does not make us timid, but gives us power, love and self-discipline.

Hebrews 6:11-12 We want each of you to show this same diligence to the very end, so that what you hope for may be fully realised. We do not want you to become lazy, but to imitate those who through faith and patience inherit what has been promised.

Hebrews 10: 36 You need to persevere so that when you have done the will of God, you will receive what he has promised.

Hebrews 11:1 Now faith is the assurance (the confirmation, the title deed) of the things [we] hope for, being the proof of things [we] do not see and the conviction of their reality [faith perceiving as real fact what is not revealed to the senses].

Hebrews 12: 1-3 Therefore, since we are surrounded by such a great cloud of witnesses, let us throw off everything that hinders and the sin that so easily entangles. And let us run with perseverance the race marked out for us, fixing our eyes on Jesus, the pioneer and perfecter of faith. For the joy set before him he endured the cross, scorning its shame, and sat down at the right hand of the throne of God. Consider him who endured such opposition from sinners, so that you will not grow weary and lose heart.

James 5:7 Be patient, then, brothers and sisters, until the Lord's coming. See how the farmer waits for the land to yield its valuable crop, patiently waiting for the autumn and spring rains.

1 Peter 1:7-9 These have come so that the proven genuineness of your faith—of greater worth than gold, which perishes even though refined by fire—may result in praise, glory and honour when Jesus Christ is revealed. Though you have not seen him, you love him; and even though you do not see him now, you believe in him and are filled with an inexpressible and glorious joy, for you are receiving the end result of your faith, the salvation of your souls.

1 John 5:4 For everyone born of God overcomes the world. This is the victory that has overcome the world, even our faith.

Scriptures on health:

Psalm 16:9 Therefore my heart is glad and my tongue rejoices; my body also will rest secure.

Psalm 77:11-13 I will remember the deeds of the LORD; yes, I will remember your miracles of long ago. I will consider all your works and meditate on all your mighty deeds. Your ways, God, are holy. What god is as great as our God?

Proverbs 10:22 The blessing of the LORD brings wealth, without painful toil for it.

Isaiah 53:4-5 Surely he took up our infirmities and carried our sorrows, yet we considered him stricken by God, smitten by him, and afflicted. But He was pierced for our transgressions, He was crushed for our iniquities; the punishment that brought us peace was on Him, and by His wounds we are healed.

Romans 6:4-5 We were therefore buried with him through baptism into death in order that, just as Christ was raised from the dead through the glory of the Father, we too may live a new life. For if we have been united with him in a death like his, we will certainly also be united with him in a resurrection like his.

Romans 8:11 And if the Spirit of him who raised Jesus from the dead is living in you, he who raised Christ from the dead will also give life to your mortal bodies because of his Spirit who lives in you.

Galatians 3:13 Christ redeemed us from the curse of the law by becoming a curse for us, for it is written: "Cursed is everyone who is hung on a pole."

Philippians 3:20-21 But our citizenship is in Heaven. And we eagerly await a Saviour from there, the Lord Jesus Christ, who, by the power that enables him to bring everything under his control, will transform our lowly bodies so that they will be like his glorious body.

1 Thessalonians 5:10-11 He died for us so that, whether we are awake or asleep, we may live together with him. Therefore encourage one another and build each other up, just as in fact you are doing.

2 Timothy 2:11-13 Here is a trustworthy saying: If we died with him, we will also live with him; if we endure, we will also reign with him. If we disown him, he will also disown us; if we are faithless, he remains faithful, for he cannot disown himself.

3 John 1:2 Dear friend, I pray that you may enjoy good health and that all may go well with you, even as your soul is getting along well.

Revelation 12:11 They triumphed over him by the blood of the Lamb and by the word of their testimony.

Revelation 22:3-4 No longer will there be any curse. The throne of God and of the Lamb will be in the city, and his servants will serve him. They will see his face, and his name will be on their foreheads.

✦

19

Testimonies:

An invitation

After a c-section with my son they told me it was not possible. Well we gave birth to a 8lb 11oz beautiful girl, a water birth in a mid-wife led hospital with no pain relief and no stitches in two hours. Anything is possible with God. I've not written this to say look at me, but someone needs to read this and take hold of it for themselves! Put your trust in Jesus, He will not let you down. I promise.

Simone

From two previous painful labours I realigned my mind and heart to the truth of God's Word I invited peace instead of fear and had a one hour pain free third labour.

Rachel

I had an awesome pregnancy and a great labour. This was, I believe, due to trust. Knowing ultimately that God was in control, and that He would be with me each step of the way. I was blessed with no sickness, no real swollen ankles, (UGG boots were a blessing here too) and the labour was no way what I had suspected it would be. I felt very blessed. My second birth was unlike my first, I prayed for a quick delivery. My waters broke at three twenty and contractions were immediately one and a half minutes apart and very quickly increased to every sixty seconds. Despite this I remained calm knowing I was created to be able to do this. At four forty-five my second beautiful son was born with no complications, quickly and perfectly healthy. Just as prayed for.

Anna

During my third birth I was able to pray in the Holy Ghost and quote scripture at the onset of each contraction and then any pain would leave. My second son's birth was so traumatic and painful, I never wanted another baby and was terrified to find out I was pregnant again. I read Supernatural Childbirth and applied it with my third son and now I can't wait to have more children.

Katherine

God's been very present in all my labours (and pregnancies), with my first I was only five centimetres dilated and the baby was severely distressed, the medical staff told me I needed a caesarean but being only seventeen years old I was scared and I knew God had a plan, so I made them give me two minutes, they didn't think it'd make a difference so they agreed, I prayed for God to make a way and when they checked me a minute later I had dilated to ten centimetres! Praise Jesus. Jordayne was born but he wasn't breathing. He was blue so my husband prayed and he started breathing and his skin colour came back, a miracle indeed!

With my second I was induced early as my legs were collapsing under me with no warning. The doctors thought that it was a disc in my spine that had softened too much, I'd either be ok after he was born, or I'd never walk again. A fifty fifty chance they said. But God has a plan, after he was born my spine was fine and I am able to walk.

My third, Jyrah, was the most amazing birth as I decided to have no drugs and attempt a water birth. My contractions started at eleven thirty and he was born at about four! The shortest labour to date! God has been very, very present and involved, I wish I could tell you more but He is my everything and when He has a plan it goes through perfectly.

Kai-Di

My labour and delivery with my second child was an extremely peaceful and grace-filled one. God's presence was there in our home as I faced the great challenge of bring our little girl into the world. Inspired by Philippa-Jo's story of how God intervened supernaturally during her own labour and delivery, I knew the Holy Spirit would be close to me during this time. As I faced each contraction I could sense Jesus was very close to me, sometimes I could even picture him standing behind me, hugging me and whispering gentle words of support and encouragement into my ears. I know now, to a much deeper level, how true it is that I can do ALL THINGS through Christ who strengthens me!

Tessa

I was one week overdue with my son, this being my first pregnancy. I had been told many stories, mostly negative, about labour, miscarrying etc. I read Supernatural Childbirth and knowing that God was involved from conception to delivery was the greatest feeling ever. I had people giving me the "pftttt, you really think that's going to help you, God designed childbirth to be painful etc." So I just ignored it, I had a great pregnancy (besides the heartburn), no vomiting, my emotions were fine, then came d-day. I was so excited to meet my son. I had my christian music going on, and my mum had prayed over me that God would be in the whole labour and that He'd guide me through and give me a spirit of power, love and a sound mind, not a spirit of fear. The first two hours I had no pain relief, the next five hours I used gas but still felt like the same as before, the next five hours I got an epidural. I still felt the contractions through that so they had to triple dose me on it, some mothers might think twelve hours is long and annoying, but I just consider how very blessed I was to experience every bit of birth. My cervix did not dilate past three and a half centimetres and he wasn't facing the right way for delivery so it resulted in a c-section, my son was born, nine pounds, three ounces and a healthy one at that, no complications. I believe God was in it the whole time. I had a fantastic anaesthetist, great midwives, great support people and although I was maxed out on a drug that would increase the contractions to maximum intensity, to regulate them it wasn't painful but intense, there's a fine line between the two I would say, but I enjoyed the whole experience and the c-section went great and healed great too. So my experience for a supernatural birth, although it may of seemed really complicated, long and annoying I believe God was in it the whole time, and the fact I even conceived through the pill.

Lizzie

When my wife gave birth to our first son, God was definitely there! Jesus was calming my wife in a supernatural way and you could find my wife singing songs of praise to God in the labour waiting room and God giving words of encouragement from the Bible to her. With our second son, God was making her very calm as well. Thank you Jesus for Supernatural Childbirth. We have to pray for You to open our eyes in spiritual awareness, because You are, in fact, present with every human coming into this world. ("Even the very numbers of hairs are counted by God").

Asger

My pregnancy was incredible. I threw up a total of five times only (that isn't morning sickness to me), I taught Zumba classes up until my ninth month, I had amazing energy and I didn't experience bloating, swelling or any of the other uncomfortable symptoms that others experienced. My labour on the other hand was not what I had in mind. My natural experience was great, it wasn't until I went to the hospital that I really experienced pain as I was induced and taken for a C-section without consent. However, there were times where my husband noticed contractions being off the charts intense and I didn't feel anything, so that I give to God. God still gets the glory, I have a beautiful, strong, healthy 8lb and 2oz baby.

Brenda

During my pregnancy I had swollen ankles, which disappeared within thirty minutes of praying that they'd go down. My Midwife was surprised because usually once you get swelling it stays until birth. When I was in active labour I had a strong contraction, then two weak ones, every ten minutes. The midwife said that was weird - like my body was giving me a break!

Talia

I started calling on the Lord for real at this point - "Oh Lord,...Oh God,...Oh Jesus,...Oh Father" That's when His strength really kicked in for me. I was so tired by then. His strength really is made perfect in our weakness! The nurses were all wonderful and so happy for me that we did it all with no medication or intervention. One of them mentioned that she only sees about one in a hundred women go without an epidural or other meds. Last time, although it was a much longer labour, in the beginning I was able to relax, listen to music, write in my journal. Then as the labour progressed I moved from one phase to the next with a sense of preparation for what was to come. This time it was just down to business, as if Father was saying, "you've done this before so let's just get this baby here. You already know that in MY strength, you can do it!"

Leslie

I've always had near perfect pregnancies, especially with my second; I was more at peace. I kept it more between me and God so I had less battle with believing I could have a painless birth. When the contractions started I was very, very peaceful. Contractions started to be painful later on and it was a battle with my faith, learning each time to trust God and believe that the next one will be painless. But I had a stronghold in my mind that I found hard to overcome; I was almost needing to feel the pain to know that the labour was progressing, I was almost holding onto the pain, I think it was because in my first pregnancy the labour was so long.

When the midwife came in the morning and told me that I was only two centimetres dilated I got discouraged and let fear come in my heart - then, oh then, the pain just almost instantly went from bearable to unbearable. Fear is just the worst enemy to pain free birth! I just couldn't come back to a place of faith. I just started to cry in the arms of my Father God and basically told Him I can't! But I saw God in so many details of the whole labour time. I had an amazing midwife who spoke faith the whole way into my heart. She kept saying things speaking straight into my fears and giving me hope!

During labour God also spoke to me the whole way. He spoke to me about my daughter and gave me a few encounters in the spirit. I did feel disappointed for not having a pain free birth but God kept my heart. I felt his love and Him telling me how proud He is of me and His favour and love were just on everything else that I could see. Even those little details I just couldn't not see the grace of God behind it!

Liz

My experience of supernatural birth happened by accident really. I was given the book 'Supernatural Childbirth' by a close friend at church. With my first son, I had no idea what childbirth and labour would be like and thought that I could wait until the last trimester to begin the preparation. It didn't work at all and that's when I understood it's not some magic but real practice of faith.

For our second try, we started the supernatural preparation in advance and soon fell pregnant. I looked up all the verses the book had recommended, gathered the ones that spoke to my heart, typed them up and printed them in a long strip of paper. I folded the strip into a small book and carried it everywhere. I started studying the verses, praying about them, and memorising them, too.

My husband had to go away for work on my due date and I didn't know what was going to happen. We were praying for God's grace and believed the child will come when 'Dad' was there. Our prayer was answered. A few days later contractions began, and got stronger when my husband had just arrived at the Eurostar station. When he was entering our road in a cab I called him to give the news.

We arrived at the hospital and the pain was very strong and sharp. I started screaming despite all the preparation. My husband was there with me and encouraged me to remember the verses, remember God's grace and believe in the miracle of supernatural birth. That's when I understood I had to communicate with my body and the baby. I did. I spoke to my body to contract rhythmically in harmony with the baby. The contractions were getting stronger and I realised how much it hurt. I prayed again the words I had studied and really believed in God's power.

It was amazing, the contractions came but there was no pain. Because of my thyroid condition baby's heartbeat was being monitored so the machine was telling me when I was contracting. I knew with God's wisdom that the contractions had to become stronger so I shouted for my womb to open up and the midwives who were now ready to deliver the baby were laughing. They agreed, the womb had to open.

I have to point out I was going from concentrating on how frequent and strong the contraction was, then to the painlessness of it. When I questioned whether the contractions were strong enough, bang, the severe pain would come back. I then prayed and was able to focus on painless contractions.

About three hours after I had walked into the hospital, I was ready to push – with my first child I was in the hospital for more than twenty four hours! I now had to focus on a different thing and that's when I felt the burning pain. My husband spoke about the amazing blessing the child would have if delivered into the world supernaturally. I went back to the verses and spoke to my body again then pushed with all my strength. It was tough, the push, but out came the baby and it was truly the most amazing thing I ever felt. I still can't forget what I felt in my body when our little baby Yumin came out – it was nothing I knew from this world.

InHae

I was pregnant with my fourth child and really wanted to go into labour naturally and possibly even have a home birth. I had been induced with my other three pregnancies!

As my pregnancy progressed I learnt I would need to be induced at thirty-seven weeks again. I chose to trust my Father God even though I didn't understand and prepared myself by getting into a place of peace and joy allowing Father God to fight for me. This wasn't easy but I know I wouldn't have experienced the birth I had if I hadn't!

I had to wait until eight o'clock in the evening to be induced but kept thanking Father God for His favour and for His Holy Spirit presence. I was given a private room and the Holy Spirit really came into the room with His joy. The midwife, myself and my friend just laughed and laughed and it changed the atmosphere in the room - joy made the way.

I was induced with the twenty-four hour induction tablet which would be pulled out if my body kicked in and began to contract by itself. Within two hours my body was contracting so strongly I was having contractions every two to three minutes so the midwife pulled the tablet out. I was three centimeters dilated and my contractions continued naturally. The friends I had praying for me had no idea that what they were praying was actually happening: my body continuing into natural labour without the drugs!

The contractions were very intense as I was having four to six contractions in ten minutes. I started to thank God for who He was and speak His goodness through all the contractions. Though the contractions were intense I had no pain as I focused on Jesus. I had never had a pain free birth before as I was always in fear but this was so different as joy had started the labour and by staying in Father God's favour and peace I experienced intensity but no pain.

The birth progressed very quickly and by five centimetres I was moved into the labour ward. My husband arrived as he had gone home to look after the children as we didn't think it was going to happen so quickly. He arrived as the midwives said it was ok for me to push! With the first push our son's head came out and with the second push our son Daniel was born!

I was in such awe at God's faithfulness and goodness to me! This was the first birth that was pain free. I didn't tear, I had a healthy baby and an amazing joyfully induced birth.

Tandy

 *Prayer*

I pray that your journey through pregnancy will take you to new heights of relationship with God and increased faith in who He is. I pray that your relationship with God will grow stronger as you seek to know Him, and as you know Him, I pray that you will know what you can experience through Him. I pray over you grace and peace for the duration of your pregnancy and Shalom in your body throughout pregnancy and labour. I pray a blessing over you to succeed in every faith venture you undertake. Jesus I ask you to journey along with this lady and let her be aware of your enduring presence. I break off you every false expectation and every previous bad experience surrounding childbearing. May you step into a new determination from a place of His rest. I pray that you are surrounded in a feeling of great expectation, that faith will rise up afresh on the inside of you. My prayer is that you will become a joyful mother of children.

Amen

Endnotes

Title	Author	Source
1: Supernatural Childbirth Page 12	Jackie Mize	Harrison House May 2010
2: When you see the invisible, you can do the impossible Page 111	Oral Roberts	Destiny Image Publishers 2005
3: Quoted on Page 127	Thomas Edison	1877
4: Cloudless Sky Page 130	Bill Johnson	Podcast: Bethel Church California
All Biblical background and references	Strongs online concordance	eliyah.com/lexicon
Some of the tools in this book are influenced by techniques used by Bethel Sozo	Dawna De Silver & Teresa Leapshire	Bethel Church, Redding California. See bethelsozo.com for further details.
Biblical quotes throughout	The Message Bible, Eugene H. Peterson New International Version New King James New Living Translation	biblegateway.com

✦

I hope that reading this book has 'spiked' your faith to a new level. I encourage you to use the journal that was written to go alongside this book to help you maintain this new faith level and grapple through His promises on a personal level. I would love to hear from you so please connect further via:

Pregnancyinhispresence.com

facebook.com/pregnancyinhispresence

twitter.com/prespregnancy

✦

Made in the USA
Charleston, SC
30 July 2014